101 Property Tax Secrets Revealed 2015/16

By

Jennifer Adams

Publisher Details

This guide is published by Tax Insider Ltd, 3 Sanderson Close, Warrington WA5 3LN.

'101 Property Tax Secrets Revealed' first published in November 2012, second edition May 2013, third edition June 2014, fourth edition November 2015.

Contents

Contents

Chapter 3.   Capital Allowances

Chapter 4.   Use Of Losses

About This Guide

The past ten years have seen property ownership change beyond all recognition. Low interest rates and the unpopularity of pension schemes have meant that many investors are looking for higher returns and are turning to property rental to provide that return.

Whatever the return on the investment anyone owning a UK property needs to factor in tax payable. All property owners will, at some time or other, find themselves subject to tax on that property. If the property is rented out income tax may be payable, if sold possibly capital gains tax and/or stamp duty land tax charged, whilst on death inheritance tax may be levied. Developers will be subject to value added tax on the construction of buildings.

However, there is much that can be done to save or at least reduce the amount of tax payable; this guide contains 101 such tax savings tips (secrets).

The tips in this guide are intended to demonstrate areas where tax savings may be possible, the actual amount being dependent upon the precise circumstances of the situation and as such the examples are included as a guide only.

Due to the restrictive number of pages, this book can only show some areas where tax planning is possible. More 'Tax Secrets' can be found in the monthly magazine Property Tax Insider and on the Tax Insider website. It must be stressed that professional advice should always be sought when undertaking any form of tax planning.

Finally, the tax allowances and rates used in examples relate to the tax year 2015/16.

Chapter 1.
Different Ways Of Owning Property

1.   Sole Investor
2.   Joint Investors
3.   Company
4.   Dealer Or Investor?
5.   Joint Ownership
6.   Profit Allocation – Calculation
7.   Joint Spouse/Civil Partnership Ownership (1)
8.   Joint Spouse/Civil Partnership Ownership (2)
9.   Joint Non-Spouse/Civil Partnership Ownership
10. Agreements On Transfer

1.   Sole Investor

The vast majority of UK properties are privately owned and many have been purchased as an investment rather than as a main residence.

A 'sole investor' is an individual who buys properties in his or her own name. The investor landlord is taxed on the amount of letting income received less allowable expenses incurred, as well as any capital gain that may be made on sale. Inheritance tax may be payable on the value of the property held at the date of death.

Non-tax reasons for buying property as a sole investor:

- There is no partner with whom to share the investment.
- The owner remains in control of the investment, making his or her own decisions without having to consult another.

Tax position: If the landlord has no other income, the annual personal allowance is deducted from any profit made on the letting income in full. If he or she has other income, the personal allowance is not available and the profits made are taxed at the landlord's marginal rate of tax.

Dependent upon the level of letting profit, being a sole investor could be expensive in comparison with joint investor ownership. A sole investor will be taxed in full at his or her marginal rate of tax whereas with joint investor ownership, the letting profit is halved with each owner's share of profit being taxed at his or her respective marginal rate. Therefore, should one investor be a basic rate taxpayer and the other a higher or additional rate taxpayer the total tax bill will be reduced by 50% of the difference between the tax due at the higher and lower rates.

Further tax reduction is possible should one investor be a non-taxpayer as the full amount of that individual's personal allowance will be available for offset.

Sole Investor

Joanne and Robert are married and own a rental property 50:50. Joanne has no other income but Robert is a 45% (additional) rate taxpayer. For the year 2015/16 the net rental profit is £825 per month – £9,900 per tax year.

Joanne: No tax liability as £9,900 x 50% = £4,950 (less than the personal allowance of £10,600).

Robert: Tax liability of £2,227.50 (£4,950 @ 45%).

If Joanne owned the property in her own name as a sole investor there would be no tax liability on the full profit (£9,900 being less than the personal allowance). This would result in a tax saving of £2,227.50.

2.   Joint Investors

Joint ownership exists where two or more persons own property together.

Therefore individuals who purchase property jointly intending to rent for the long term are 'joint investors' being taxed on their share of the annual rental profits made or gains made on sale. Joint owners of property purchased with the intention to sell after restoration are likely to be in a 'trading partnership' with each being taxed as a self-employed 'property dealer'.

The difference between joint investors and a trading partnership is that for a partnership to exist there needs to be a degree of organisation similar to that required for an ordinary commercial business with a view to making a profit. A partnership agreement is therefore recommended.

Non-tax reasons for buying as joint investors:

- Sharing of the investment.
- Control and running of the properties is shared.
- If owned as joint tenants (see Tip 5), on death the property is transferred automatically to the joint investor owner who may not be one's next of kin.
- Funding for the investment is not possible as a sole investor.

Tax position: Correct tax planning can enable the reduction of the total tax liability. The letting profit is divided with each owner's share of the profit being taxed at his or her respective marginal rate. The example shows the tax position should one owner be taxed at a higher rate than the other.

Joint Investors

Joanne and Robert are married and own a portfolio of rental properties 50:50.

For the year 2015/16 Joanne is a basic rate taxpayer but Robert is a 45% additional rate taxpayer. Total net rental profit is £825 per month, i.e. £9,900 per year = £4,950 each.

Joanne: Tax liability of £990 (£4,950 @ 20%).

Robert: Tax liability of £2,227.50 (£4,950 @ 45%).

If Robert owned the properties as a sole investor the tax liability would be £4,455; by owning the properties jointly with Joanne there is a tax saving of £1,237.50. (The saving could be even higher, should the property be solely in Joanne's name.)

3.   Company

There are different types of company but the one most commonly used for property tax planning is the private company limited by shares. Shareholders are the owners of the company, which is administered by directors (who may also be the shareholders).

Non-tax reasons for buying as a company:

- A limited company is a separate legal entity from the shareholders.
- Profits and losses belong to the company.
- The company can continue regardless of the death, resignation or bankruptcy of the shareholders or directors.
- The liability of shareholders is limited to the amount unpaid (if any) on the shares held.
- If the company fails, the shareholders are not normally required to make good the deficit (unless personal guarantees have been given).
- A company may find it easier to raise finance.

Tax position: The corporation tax rate for 2015/16 is 20%. Although companies do not have a personal allowance, if the profits from a property business owned by individual(s) are charged at the higher personal tax rates, it could potentially be more beneficial for the properties to be held inside a company.

4.   Dealer Or Investor?

Difference

Anyone buying property to let out on a long-term basis will most likely be deemed an investor, whereas someone buying to refurbish then sell, whether resulting in a gain or not, may be deemed to be dealing or trading in properties and be taxed accordingly. The two main factors to consider are *intention* and whether the transaction has the characteristics of being a trade.

Capital/investment transaction

Unless losses are incurred on sale, it is usually preferable for a transaction to be of a capital/investment nature and for the property to be held personally or via a joint/partnership investment, rather than held within a company. This is because individuals are allowed an annual exempt amount on sale and may be charged a lower effective rate of capital gains tax than the tax rates charged on company profits.

Property dealing/trading transaction

If the transaction is in a property dealing/trading situation and the property owner is taxed at the higher rates, it may be preferable for the property to be owned within a company rather than individually because the overall tax rates charged through corporate ownership can be lower than the income tax rates on trading profits.

A particular problem may arise for those engaged in the property business in some way (e.g. a builder, surveyor or estate agent). Even though the purchase itself has nothing to do with their trade HMRC could try to argue that the purchase of land and subsequent sale is a trading transaction.

5.   Joint Ownership

Legally speaking, the two ways in which property may be held jointly are as:

- Joint tenants – each owner has equal rights over the property; when one dies the property is automatically transferred into the other owner's name.
- Tenants in common – the share of each owner is separate, may be unequal and may be disposed of in lifetime or on death as the respective owner wishes.

Persons who own property on their own do so in their sole name with sole rights.

Spouses/civil partners can own property in their own names or jointly, usually as joint tenants.

Two or more unmarried persons may own property either as joint tenants or tenants in common, although it is more usual to be held as tenants in common.

6.   Profit Allocation – Calculation

Unless the owners are married a property owned jointly, or held within a partnership business proper does not mean that the rental profit or loss must be allocated in the same proportion as the underlying ownership. Rather, the owners can agree a different split as they see fit, the proportion referring to profits and losses only and not necessarily to the capital received should the property be sold.

Profit Allocation – Calculation

The purchase deed of 54 Dorchester Place shows that the property ownership is split 90:10 between John and his partner, Jane. For the tax year 2015/16 the net rental profit is £14,200 per year. John is a higher rate taxpayer whilst Jane is a student with no income other than her share of the profit.

John's annual tax bill is £5,112 on his 90% share (£14,200 x 90% @ 40% = £5,112); Jane has no tax to pay on her 10% share (£14,200 x 10% = £1,420) as this amount is less than the personal allowance.

Joint net amount remaining after tax = £14, 200 – £5,112 = £9,088.

It would be more beneficial for the 90:10 split to be in Jane's favour as this would mean a tax bill for John of £568 (£14,200 x 10% @ 40% = £568) and nil for Jane.

Joint net amount remaining after tax = £14,200 – £568 = £13,632.

There would be a tax saving of £4,544.

7. Joint Spouse/Civil Partnership Ownership (1)

By default, rental profit from property jointly owned by spouses/civil partners is taxed 50:50 irrespective of the underlying respective proportion of actual ownership. This does not apply to property held within a business partnership proper. However, if it would be more income tax efficient for the split of profit to be different, then the profit may be divided according to actual ownership once HMRC has been notified. A couple may change the underlying ownership to suit, but note that such unequal ownership can be achieved only as 'tenants in common'.

Most importantly, a Form 17 *'Declaration of beneficial interest in joint property and income'* must be filed with HMRC within 60 days of the date of signature (this restriction is strictly applied).

Evidence of beneficial interests in the property being unequal must be submitted with the signed Form 17 in all cases (e.g. the signing of a declaration of trust or a deed of arrangement).

The declaration comes into effect from the date of signature (i.e. it cannot be back dated) and remains in place until a replacement form is submitted. A replacement form will be required either when the interests in the property or income change, or the owners stop living together as a married couple/civil partners or one of the joint owners dies. Even the smallest change in interest cancels the declaration and without submission of a subsequent form the 50:50 split will automatically apply. On death or permanent separation the income is split as to the beneficial interest.

Joint Spouse/Civil Partnership Ownership (1)

Andrew and Anne are married and jointly own a rented property. Andrew is a 45% additional rate taxpayer and Anne is a 20% basic rate taxpayer. Their accountant has calculated that it would be more beneficial for the profit to be split 80:20 to ensure that the least income tax is paid.

The legal ownership is therefore changed to being held 80:20 as 'tenants in common' and the declaration Form 17 signed, but unfortunately is not submitted within the 60-day time limit.

The income tax split therefore remains at 50:50 but legally the underlying ownership has changed to 80:20. The 50:50 tax split will remain until a fresh Form 17 is submitted.

8.   Joint Spouse/Civil Partnership Ownership (2)

If one spouse/civil partner owns a rental property solely in their own name but is a higher or additional rate taxpayer and the other spouse/civil partner is not, it would be beneficial for at least some of the rental profit to be taxed on the spouse/civil partner.

To alter the income tax percentage charged, ownership of part of the property must be transferred into the other spouse/civil partner's name.

However, should the owning spouse/civil partner not wish to transfer any material percentage ownership but still wish to reduce their tax bill, a nominal amount of, say, 1% could be transferred.

In this instance the HMRC Form 17 *'Declaration of beneficial interest in joint property and income'* must **not** be signed because not signing will ensure that the underlying property ownership is (say) 99:1 but the income split is 50:50.

Joint Spouse/Civil Partnership Ownership (2)

Andrew and Anne are married. Andrew owns a property yielding £8,000 rental income annually. Andrew is a 45% additional rate taxpayer and Anne is a non-taxpayer.

Andrew transfers 1% of the property ownership to Anne, retaining 99%.

Unless a Form 17 is validly submitted each is subsequently taxed on 50% of the income.

As Anne is a non-taxpayer, this will produce a tax saving of £1,800.

---

9. Joint Non-Spouse/Civil Partnership Ownership

If a property is owned jointly by two persons who are not married or in a civil partnership, the rental profit is **not** automatically split 50:50.

Rather, the income split is in whatever proportion they agree between themselves.

The HMRC Form 17 *'Declaration of beneficial interest in joint property and income'* is **not** relevant in this instance but a written agreement would be helpful.

10. Agreements On Transfer

The transfer of legal ownership of a property is confirmed by the signing of a written agreement. Agreements are per share of property and not one per property.

Agreements On Transfer

Jack and Jill are married and jointly own a Buy to Let property, with no mortgage. They wish to gift 1% of the property to each of their two adult children (new share of property being 49:49:1:1), the rental income and expenses to be shared 50:50 between the adult children only. What are the practicalities?

To enable the transfer Jack and Jill need to hold the property as 'tenants in common' thus ensuring that each of their respective shares can be disposed of to whomever and in whatever proportion each wishes.

They can then transfer 1% each, i.e. 1% to one child and 1% to the other. Two written agreements will be required, one to confirm each transfer.

The net profit split will be a separate matter being in whatever proportions the new owners agree between themselves.

However, the amendment to the net profit allocation should also be confirmed.

Chapter 2.
Letting Accounts

11. Record Keeping

UK-resident landlords are generally taxed on rental profits made wherever the properties are situated in the world.

A record of the rental income, expenses incurred and capital items purchased must be kept. Separate sets of records are needed if the properties are let as 'furnished holiday lets' because these properties are taxed under different tax rules.

Keep:

- invoices, expense and capital item receipts, rental statements, mortgage statements;
- past years' income and expenditure accounts and Tax Returns submitted;
- bank statements;
- details of purchase of property – date of acquisition, purchase price including associated costs;
- details of subsequent improvement costs; and
- if the property was previously the landlord's main residence, details of periods when the landlord lived in the property and of periods let – to ensure Principal Private Residence and letting reliefs are correctly claimed on sale.

NOTE: In the Tribunal case of *Ridpath* (*Ridpath v HMRC* (2013) TC02785) it was accepted that a total of £40,000 had likely been incurred on property improvements. However, the claim was disallowed because it was impossible to define precisely how much had actually been spent as there was no proof of the expenditure.

Record Keeping

Keep records manually, using spreadsheets or software packages, for example:

- Landlords Property Manager
  www.propertyportfoliosoftware.co.uk
- Landlord Vision
  www.landlordvision.co.uk

HMRC have an index of the record-keeping requirements for a business available on the GOV.UK website at www.gov.uk/keeping-your-pay-tax-records/rental-income.

A penalty of up to £3,000 can be imposed by HMRC for failure to maintain adequate records for self-assessment purposes.

12. Revenue v Capital Expenditure

In calculating the profit or loss of a rental business the on-going costs of renting a property (agents' fees, repairs, insurance, etc.) being 'revenue costs' are allowable immediately as a deduction against rental income received.

No deductions are allowed for capital expenditure but capital allowances may be claimed to take into account the depreciation of some capital assets used.

Ascertaining whether a cost is revenue or capital expense can be difficult, but HMRC have published a Toolkit which is in the format of questions to help in deciding under which heading the expenditure may be allowed.

Revenue v Capital Expenditure

The current edition of HMRC's Toolkit 'Capital v Revenue Expenditure' is dated June 2015.

The weblink is:
https://www.gov.uk/government/publications/hmrc-capital-vs-revenue-expenditure-toolkit

13. Property Deposits

The usual practice when letting a property is for a tenant to pay a deposit to a landlord before moving into the property. The deposit is returned at the end of the tenancy, subject to any deductions for 'dilapidations', i.e. any repairs that the tenant has not undertaken although contractually obliged to do so.

On payment the landlord has no legal right over the deposit money; he or she is only entitled to some or all of the deposit at the end of the tenancy.

The tax position is that a deposit is income to be included in the letting accounts. However the inclusion in the accounts is deferred until the landlord acquires the right to retain some or all of the deposit, which is usually at the end of the tenancy. It is at that point that the amount of deposit retained is brought into the accounts as income and the cost of repair as an expense.

The repair costs may be greater than the deposit. In this situation the tenant may pay the landlord compensation in addition to the amount of deposit. This additional amount is treated as income if the landlord subsequently re-lets the property.

However, if the landlord does not subsequently re-let then the payment is treated as a capital receipt.

14. 'Duality Of Purpose'

Expenses incurred in the running of a property letting business are deductible from rental income received in calculating the taxable profit. However, just because a payment has been made, it does not necessarily mean that it will be allowable.

Strictly, for an expense to be allowed the business purpose must be the sole purpose; there must be no dual reason for the expense. Where it is difficult to split the business element from any private element then the whole expense amount is usually disallowed.

In practice, however, some 'dual purpose'-type expenses may be permitted. The expense usually quoted is of expenses incurred on running a car used partly for business and partly for private purposes, the business part obviously being allowed.

Duality Of Purpose

James rents out his former main residence in Manchester whilst he is working away from home in Brighton. Every month he travels by car to Manchester to view the property. His mother lives in the vicinity and he sometimes combines the trip with a visit to his mother.

On these occasions all expenditure might be denied because of the 'dual purpose'.

On the trips James undertakes for the sole reason of visiting the property, the costs incurred are allowable in full. The calculation of use of petrol is straightforward (see Tip 15). However, there will be 'duality of purpose' with reference to such costs as insurance and servicing. A proportion may be claimed, but an element would be disallowed as being incurred for personal use as James uses the car for reasons other than solely viewing the property.

15. Car Expenses

The cost of running a vehicle used in a letting business can be claimed against rental income. Unless the vehicle is used solely for business purposes, the costs must be apportioned between private and business use.

There are two alternative methods of calculation:

1. Note the recorded mileage on 6 April each year giving the total mileage over the full tax year. Record the mileage of every business-related trip made in the tax year, which will give the proportion of running costs to claim.
2. A business with annual turnover of less than the VAT registration limit (£82,000 for the tax year 2015/16) can claim 45p for the first 10,000 business miles incurred and 25p for any additional miles.

Whichever method is used, once used, it cannot be changed until the vehicle itself is changed.

Car Expenses

James travels 12,000 miles on business attending to his portfolio of properties. The total recorded mileage (including private journeys) for the year is 15,000. Total cost of running the car is £3,750 per year.

Method 1: £3,750 x 12,000/15,000 = £3,000

Method 2: (10,000 x 45p) + (2,000 x 25p) = £5,000

Method 2 will produce the most tax-efficient amount to claim.

---

16. Travel Expenses

The cost of business-related travel in attending to rental properties is allowable as an expense for tax purposes; any travel costs incurred for personal reasons are not.

Travel costs in attending foreign let property can also be claimed providing that there is no 'duality of purpose' (i.e. a visit is made to the property at the same time as being on holiday).

Travel Expenses

John owns a portfolio of properties in the UK and Spain. He is interested in expanding his portfolio into Portugal.

Whilst on holiday in Spain he visits the Spanish property for its annual visit and also flies to Portugal to view a potential property before flying back to Spain to finish his holiday. He then returns to the UK from Spain.

The travel costs of car parking, petrol, the return flight to Spain and then back to the UK will not be allowed as there is a 'duality of purpose' of the holiday.

The similar costs of the flight, etc. from Spain to Portugal will be allowed in full as being incurred solely in relation to the rental business.

17. Legal Fees

Expenditure on professional fees is deductible from the rental income of a property as revenue expenditure if incurred for the purposes of the rental business. Fees incurred in relation to the purchase and/or sale of a property are deductible as capital expenditure on disposal of the property in the capital gains tax calculation.

Specific legal costs allowed as revenue expenditure:

- Fees incurred on the renewal of a lease if the lease is for less than 50 years (except for any proportion that relates to the payment of a premium on the renewal of a lease).
- Expenses incurred in connection with the first letting if it is for a tenure of less than a year (includes the cost of drawing up the lease, agents' and surveyors' fees and commission).
- Expenses incurred on preparing a replacement short lease where it closely follows a previous agreement.
- Costs in relation to rent arbitration and evicting of an unsatisfactory tenant so as the property can be re-let.

Specific legal costs allowed as capital expenditure:

- Generally, costs are deemed to be a capital expense if they relate to a capital item, such as the actual purchase or sale of the property.

18. Allowable Interest

Any business owner taking out a mortgage/loan in order to finance capital to invest in a business is allowed to deduct interest paid from income received.

Renting is deemed to be a 'business' in the taxman's eyes for income tax purposes. The 'capital' investment is the property itself. Any mortgage interest paid is deductible from rental income received but restricted to the market value of the property if originally not purchased with a view to rent.

Should an owner not use all of the available capital, the interest remains fully allowable (assuming that what is used, is used only for business purposes) because the original reason for the mortgage remains, namely to invest capital in the business in order to finance the purchase of property.

The loan does not need to be in the form of a mortgage secured on the property itself. Interest on a personal loan (even via use of a credit card) or secured on another property is deductible from the rental income received.

If cash is used to finance the purchase initially and then the property is mortgaged to replace the cash, the interest paid on the mortgage will be allowable in full against the rental income when received.

The reason for the interest payments being allowed is *'intention'* – the intention being to purchase the property via a mortgage, the cash being used merely in place of a bridging loan.

Planning Point: For landlords, interest relief at the higher rates of tax is being phased out over a four-year period as from 6 April 2017 such that by the tax year 2020/21 only basic rate relief will be claimable. The relief will be given as a reduction on the lower of the interest affected, the rental profits, and the individual's income (excluding savings and dividend income) for the tax year.

19.   Equity Release

Income tax relief is available on a loan taken out to release capital in a rented property that is subsequently used to purchase another property or even to reduce the capital outstanding on the main residence. The actual reason for the mortgage is irrelevant.

The key criterion is that the total amount of capital released must not exceed the market value of the property when originally brought into the letting business. If the property had originally been bought with the intention to let then this amount would be the purchase price; otherwise use the market value at the date of transfer.

Planning Point: As from 6 April 2017 interest relief at higher rates of tax is being phased out over a four-year period such that by the tax year 2020/21 only basic rate relief will be claimable.

Equity Release

Anne wishes to raise £150,000 via a mortgage on two Buy To Let properties that were purchased with cash some years ago. The purchase price of the properties was £125,000 and they were let out immediately on acquisition. The mortgage monies will be used as capital to purchase a holiday cottage for personal use.

The maximum amount of interest deductible will be the proportion relating to the amount paid for the properties originally, i.e. £125,000.

There is no need to include the cottage in the portfolio for tax relief to be allowed. It can be kept for private use but interest on £25,000 (the balance of the £150,000 mortgage) will be disallowed.

20.   Portfolio Mortgages

Tax relief is allowed on interest paid on mortgages/loans taken out to finance the purchase of assets held within a business. Landlords who own two or more properties are deemed to own a 'portfolio' of business assets.

Lenders have designed products that treat the 'portfolio' as one single business account regardless of the number of properties purchased or whether the full amount of capital has been utilised. The individual properties may have separate mortgages each with different interest rates charged but the 'portfolio' is treated as one single business account. 'One portfolio' means one agreement, one monthly payment and one mortgage statement.

Should not all of the capital be used, tax relief on interest payments is still fully allowable because the original reason for the mortgage/loan remains, namely to finance the use of capital by a property business.

Planning Point: As from 6 April 2017 tax relief at higher rates on interest paid is being phased out over a four-year period such that by the tax year 2020/21 only basic rate relief will be claimable.

Portfolio Mortgages

Avril owns six properties with a total value of £2m. With a portfolio mortgage outstanding of £1.7m there is a 'shortfall' of £300,000. This amount is not the equity found in any one property, but in the portfolio spread over the six properties.

Therefore £300,000 is available for further investment; the interest will be fully tax deductible.

21.   Loan Finance Costs

Interest on a loan used to buy a property for letting is an allowable expense against the rental income as is interest on a loan taken out for repairs.

The costs of obtaining loan finance are also allowable. Dependent on the type of loan obtained, the following are tax deductible:

- Legal and professional expenses for the negotiation of a loan and preparing documents.
- Underwriting commissions, brokerage and introduction fees.
- Land registry fees, search fees and valuers' fees in connection with the security of the loan.
- Commitment fees for an undertaking to make the loan available.
- Costs of replacing or varying a loan.

Some lenders add the costs of setting up the loan to the loan itself. Provided these costs are allowable, the interest associated on the relevant part of the loan is also allowable.

A lender usually charges a penalty on the early repayment of the loan. HMRC accepts this as a cost relating to the loan itself and it is therefore deductible as an expense against income.

If the expense is deemed not income tax deductible this does not necessarily mean that no relief is available. It may be possible to claim against capital gains tax when the property is eventually sold.

22. Repairs, Replacements And Renewals

Work carried out to an existing or newly acquired property resulting in the property being improved or altered is deemed to be a capital expense, which is deductible in the capital gains calculation on sale.

Repairs such as painting and redecorating, mending broken windows, replacing tiles, etc. are an allowable deduction from the rental income.

If a business rents a commercial property and under the terms of the lease the tenant is required to incur the cost of repairs, then the expense is allowed against the profits of the tenant's business in full as the cost is required to enable the business to continue.

Currently landlords of unfurnished lettings are permitted to claim under the 'renewals' basis whereby the cost of replacements or 'renewals' of items such as a cooker can be deducted from rental profit so long as the cost of the original item had not been claimed. A claim might be possible as 'repairs' if the item repaired is attached to the fabric of the building and providing the item is 'like for like'. Therefore the replacement of items such as sinks, baths and radiators should be allowed.

Planning Point: As from 6 April 2016 a new 'replacement furniture relief' will be available whereby landlords of all properties (apart from furnished holiday lets) can claim a deduction for the capital cost of replacing furniture, furnishings, appliances and kitchenware provided for the tenants' use. The claim will be allowed so long as the original cost has not previously been claimed.

Claims for relief as 'repairs' will remain on items attached to the fabric of the building.

23. 'Wear And Tear' Allowance

Currently a 'Wear and Tear' allowance can only be claimed on rental property that is let as fully furnished, that is when the property includes such items as a cooker, fridge, sofa, etc.

The allowance cannot be claimed on unfurnished or partly furnished properties. The usual 'test' of status is whether the tenant can walk into the property and live there immediately. It would also confirm the situation if the lease included the word 'furnished'.

The claim is an annual allowance calculated as 10% of the net rental received after deducting any costs paid for by the landlord, which are normally the tenant's burden – such as council tax. This is a valuable relief as it means that tax relief is available without any actual expenditure having been made.

Planning Point: At the time of publishing the result of an HMRC consultation is awaited. In the consultation titled 'Replacing Wear and Tear Allowance with Tax Relief for Replacing Furnishings in Let Residential Dwelling Houses', it is proposed that as from 6 April 2016 the 'Wear and Tear' allowance will be replaced by a new relief (the 'Replacement Furniture Relief') and be available to all let properties apart from furnishing holiday lets.

Under this relief the cost of replacement furniture will be allowed and the 10% claim will be no more, which may increase the tax due for those landlords of furnished properties who usually claimed the 10% relief. This does, however, introduce a planning opportunity for such landlords – just for the 2015/16 and 2016/17 tax years as shown in the example.

'Wear And Tear' Allowance

John lets out a fully furnished property at a rent of £600 per month. Out of this £600 he pays £100, being the cost of the utility bills and the gardener each month.

He incurred no expenditure during the tax year 2014/15 and as such was allowed to claimed the 'Wear and Tear' allowance as follows:

Annual income = (£600 – £100 per month) x 12 months = £6,000.

Claim: £6,000 x 10% = £600.

Planning Point: John was intending not to incur expenditure for the tax year 2015/16. However following the tenant leaving on 20 March 2016 John found that he would have to replace the cooker.

If John delays purchase of the cooker until after 6 April 2016 he will be able to claim the 10% 'Wear and Tear' Allowance for 2015/16 and then also claim for the cost of the replacement cooker on his Tax Return for 2016/17.

24. Pre-Letting Expenses

Expenses may be incurred in the setting up of a letting business before the first rental receipt is received (for example, travel, phone, advertising, etc.). If so, deduction from rental income may be possible once the letting starts.

Relief is only allowable under these special rules where the expenditure is:

- incurred within a period of seven years before the date the rental business actually starts;
- is not otherwise allowable as a deduction for tax purposes (i.e. against any other income or capital gain); and
- would have been allowed as a deduction if it had been incurred after the rental business started.

Letting expenditure incurred pre-commencement is treated as having been incurred on the day on which the rental business starts and then added to other allowable letting expenses incurred during the tax year. This total amount is then deducted from the total letting receipts for that year.

The expenses must not be for the purchase of capital items. Capital expenditure is potentially deductible but there are separate rules of calculation.

Costs incurred in relation to the actual purchase of the property, including legal fees, are a capital cost allowed against the proceeds of the eventual disposal of property under the capital gains tax rules.

25.   Pre-Letting Repairs

Expenses for repair and maintenance incurred prior to the first letting income received may be allowable provided certain conditions are met, namely that:

- The cost is for the replacement of worn or dilapidated items.
- The property was in a fit state of repair for use in the letting business prior to its actually being let.
- The price paid for the property was not substantially reduced to take into account its dilapidated state of repair.
- The purchase price, if reduced, was reduced only to take into account 'normal wear and tear'.

Pre-Letting Repairs

The surveyor's report undertaken on the purchase of a property will often include an estimate of the rental income that could be derived from a property; this can be useful evidence that the property was in a 'fit state of repair' before money is spent on repairs.

Alternatively the taking of photographs before repairs are undertaken could be admitted as proof.

26.   Post-Letting Expenses

Expenses incurred in the running of a property business will have been spent in order to generate income and as such can be deducted from income received during the year.

When the letting ceases there will be no income against which relief can be claimed. However, by ensuring that any expense is accrued (allowed) for, tax relief is available; the crucial factor is not when the expense is paid or the date on the invoice but when the need for the expense arose.

Post-Letting Expenses

Last year Tony rented a property to a couple who left suddenly without giving notice. When Tony entered the property he found it in need of substantial redecoration and repair. A couple of weeks later a reminder for an unpaid electricity bill arrived. What expenses can be claimed?

Damage to property – as the property had been damaged whilst the property was let (or available to let) the expense of repair can be claimed.

Electricity bill – the bill is not Tony's legal responsibility but if he is unable to find the whereabouts of the previous tenants he will have to pay in order for the electricity supply not to be cut off. The expense is a cost of the letting and is therefore allowable.

27.   Expenses On Sale

After the decision has been made to sell a rental property, expenses incurred cannot be deducted from the rental income received after that date. Although there is no specific legal requirement for written confirmation of the date of the decision, it would be advisable to make a note.

With a portfolio of properties, expenses such as stationery, petrol, phone bill, etc. are allowable because, even after a particular property has been sold, a business will still be in place receiving income against which such costs may be deducted.

Repair costs incurred on a property that is in the process of being sold are not generally deductible against the letting income. They also cannot be utilised as capital expenditure against the sale proceeds as the cost of maintaining a capital asset is not deductible for capital gains tax purposes.

Most importantly, mortgage interest accruing after the last tenant has left and the decision has been made to sell is not tax deductible as the property no longer forms part of the letting business.

28.   Property Let At Less Than Market Rate

HMRC do not have the power to tell a landlord how much to charge for the rental of their property but they can restrict the amount of expenses claimed against any rent that is paid.

HMRC take the view that unless the landlord charges a full market rent for a property and imposes normal market lease conditions, it is unlikely that the expenses of the property are incurred 'wholly and exclusively', which is required to arrive at rental business profits. However, HMRC are prepared to allow expenses to be deducted up to the amount of rent received, thereby producing neither a profit nor a loss.

Should there be any excess expenses incurred in properties let at less than the market rent, they cannot be carried forward for deduction against rental income received in a later tax year. Losses incurred on such a property simply do not exist.

Properties let 'rent free' are regarded by HMRC as being tax neutral and outside the scope of the property income tax regime.

Property Let At Less Than Market Rate

To ensure that the property does not lose its 'business' status it needs to remain available for commercial letting even if the property is being used 'rent free' for a time.

For example, a property will be able to retain its commercial status if an owner can prove that he is actively looking for tenants but has allowed the present tenants to reside 'rent free' whilst looking for replacement paying tenants.

29. 'Rent-A-Room' Relief (1)

The 'Rent-A-Room' relief scheme is an optional tax exemption scheme that allows property owners who let out spare furnished rooms in their only or main home to receive up to £4,250 per annum gross and not be subject to tax.

If the rent received exceeds £4,250, the first £4,250 is tax free, income tax being paid on the balance. This obviously covers income from lodgers and may also be applied to bed and breakfast or guest houses which would usually be assessed as a trade.

The exemption limit of £4,250 is reduced to £2,125 if, during the tax year, someone else receives income from letting from the same property.

The £4,250 limit is not reduced if the room is let for less than 12 months. The same amount applies, therefore, even if the room is rented for only one month or just in term time.

The owner and lodger must occupy the property for at least part of the letting period in each tax year of claim.

The 'Rent-A-Room' relief limit will be increased to £7,500 as from 6 April 2016.

'Rent-A-Room' Relief (1)

Sisters Jane, Julie and Rose inherited a six-bedroom house from their father. The sisters live in the property as their main residence and it is large enough such that three of the bedrooms are let. The 'Rent-A-Room' limit is halved to £2,125 each as 'someone else received income from the same property'.

In this situation the total exemption amount is £6,375 (i.e. 3 x £2,125).

It is irrelevant that the total exemption amount exceeds the £4,250 limit.

30. 'Rent-A-Room' Relief (2)

The rules of the 'Rent-A-Room' relief scheme enable the landlord to prepare the usual income and expenditure accounts and then compare the actual expenses incurred with the 'Rent-A-Room' relief.

The default position is the normal method of calculation; should a landlord decide that 'Rent-A-Room' relief would be more beneficial he or she must make a formal claim.

A comparison can be made year on year and the method changed to cater for whichever gives the better result.

A landlord has up to one year after 31 January following the end of the tax year to decide which option to use and to make a claim.

Rent-A-Room Relief (2)

Julie is a basic rate taxpayer receiving gross income of £5,000 from letting out her spare room to include the provision of breakfast.

For 2014/15, Julie claimed 'Rent-A-Room' relief and was taxed as follows:

Gross income	£5,000
Relief	(£4,250)
Balance to be taxed	£750

Tax payable at the 20% basic rate = £150.

In the subsequent year 2015/16 Julie estimates that she will receive the same gross amount of £5,000 but will incur costs of £6,000, producing a loss of (£1,000).

Clearly, for this year, it would be more beneficial to prepare normal property income and expense accounts claiming the loss, rather than claiming 'Rent-A-Room' relief (under which she would face a tax bill as in 2014/15 above of £150 rather than being able to claim the loss of £(1,000)).

The loss can generally be claimed against other property income – or carried forward and offset against future net profits.

31. Furnished Holiday Lettings

The operation of a furnished holiday let (FHL) is deemed to be a business and not a property income investment. As such the usual business income and expenditure accounts are prepared.

Specific points:

- Accommodation must be available for short-term letting for 210 days in any one tax year and actually be let for 105 days of the year.
- Accommodation should not normally be in the same occupation for a continuous period of 31 days in a period of 155 days in any one tax year. Long-term letting should not exceed 155 days.
- The 'occupation' test can be met by making an election to average periods of occupation of any or all of the FHLs owned.
- Rent must be charged at a market rate.
- The rental profit or losses are kept separate from other non-FHL property, such that losses can only be offset against income of the same FHL business.
- Capital gains tax business asset 'roll-over' relief and 'Entrepreneurs' Relief' are potentially available.
- If the property qualified as a FHL last year but failed to do so this year because the actual occupation days were too low, an election can be made to continue to treat as a FHL this year and potentially next year.

NOTE: The new 'Replacement Furniture Relief' (see Tip 23) will not apply to FHL when the relief comes into operation on 6 April 2016.

Chapter 3.
Capital Allowances

32.   Annual Investment Allowance

Capital allowances cannot generally be claimed by landlords who let residential property. They are more likely to be claimed by landlords of commercial property (e.g. hotels), as 'plant and machinery'. The claim encompasses such assets as lifts, central heating and air-conditioning. Furnished holiday lettings are deemed to be a 'trade' and, as such, capital allowances can be claimed.

The Annual Investment Allowance (AIA) is a 100% allowance on the cost of investment in standard plant and machinery up to a set limit. For expenditure incurred before 31 December 2015 the limit is £500,000. As from 1 January 2016 the allowance has been fixed at £200,000. Expenditure in excess of the limit is dealt with under the standard 'writing down allowance' rules, any unused AIA being lost. Thus, any expenditure in excess of the AIA amount should be delayed until the next tax year.

Transitional rules apply for those companies whose tax period spans the operative date of 1 January 2016 on a proportional basis.

Annual Investment Allowance

A company has an accounting year ending 31 March 2016. On 31 July 2015 the company invested £650,000 in refurbishing a substantial apartment block of furnished holiday lettings – replacing kitchens, bathrooms and security systems.

The maximum entitlement to AIA under the transitional rules will be £425,000 (i.e. (9/12 x £500,000) + (3/12 x £200,000)).

Of the amount invested, £425,000 will be eligible for AIA, the remaining £225,000 receiving tax relief at 18% a year on a decreasing balance basis under the writing down allowance rules.

33. Writing Down Allowance (1) – Sale Of 'Pool' Assets

Capital allowances are available on the purchase of certain fixed asset items used in a letting business. Landlords who let residential property cannot generally claim capital allowances unless the property is furnished holiday accommodation or is commercially let as a hotel.

Expenditure in excess of the Annual Investment Allowance limit in respect of which AIA is not claimed, is transferred into a 'pool' and claimed ('written down') over a period of several years (generally at 18% per annum).

If any assets in the pool are subsequently sold, the proceeds are deducted from the pool amount brought forward therefore reducing the value against which further writing down allowances can be claimed.

Writing Down Allowance – Sale Of 'Pool' Assets

The brought forward balance on the capital allowances pool claim in Jane's property portfolio as at 31 March 2015 was £85,000.

Assets comprising the main pool were sold for £20,000 during the year 2015/16.

The calculation claim is:

Pool balance brought forward	£85,000
Sale of assets	£(20,000)
Balance	£65,000
Writing down allowance (18%)	£(11,700)
Balance of allowances carried forward	£53,300
Total allowances claimed	£11,700

34. Writing Down Allowance (2) – Excess Expenditure

Where the Annual Investment Allowance (AIA) is not claimed or not available because the limit has already been reached, tax relief is given on the purchase of capital items on a reducing balance termed the 'writing down allowance'.

Expenditure in excess of the AIA limit enters either the main pool or a 'special rate' pool for the purchase of integrated features and is eligible for the writing down allowance at 18% per annum (main pool) or 8% ('special rate' pool) in the accounting period.

For expenditure incurred before 31 December 2015 the limit is £500,000. As from 1 January 2016 the allowance has been fixed at £200,000. Expenditure in excess of the limit is dealt with under the standard 'writing down allowance' rules and any unused AIA is lost.

Transitional rules apply on a proportional basis for those companies whose tax period spans the operative date of 1 January 2016.

Writing Down Allowance – Excess Expenditure

In July 2015 Jane was granted planning permission to refurbish a block of flats in her portfolio of properties. At the end of the previous accounting period (5 April 2015) there was a main pool balance brought forward of £100,000. The final cost of the refurbishment totalled £630,000 all of which was incurred in October 2015.

The 2015/16 calculation will be:

Pool balance brought forward	£100,000
Additions qualifying for AIA	£630,000
AIA claim maximum	(£425,000) **
Balance allocated to main pool	£205,000
Total eligible for writing down allowance	£305,000
Writing down allowance (18%)	£(54,900)
Balance of allowances carried forward	£250,100

Total allowances claimed: £425,000 + £54,900 = £479,900

** AIA claim maximum: (£500,000 x 9/12) + (£200,000 x 3/12) = £425,000.

NOTE: Despite the fact that the overall maximum AIA for the accounting period is £425,000, if the expenditure had been incurred after 1 January 2016 the maximum that can be claimed is £50,000 (£200,000 x 3/12 = £50,000).

If Jane could defer the expenditure until after 5 April 2016 £200,000 AIA could be claimed, although in that case tax relief would be deferred for a full year.

35. Restricted Claim

Capital allowances available on assets purchased for use in a property business need not be claimed in full; the amount can be restricted by choice, if appropriate. The amount of allowances claimed in any one year can be restricted to bring the profit to the level of the personal allowance, thereby preserving the balance of allowances to be carried forward for future years.

This will be relevant if, for example, the owner's total income for the year is less than the personal allowance.

Restricted Claim

Jane's property business has a main pool written down value brought forward of £80,000. Profit for the year to 5 April 2016 is £18,600; she has no other income.

The capital allowances calculation for 2015/16 is:

Pool balance brought forward		£80,000
Writing down allowance possible at 18%	£14,400	
Amount of claim (restricted)	£(8,000)	
		£(6,400)
Balance of allowances carried forward		£73,600

The tax liability calculation is:

Profit	£18,600
Less writing down allowance claim	£(8,000)
Net profit	£10,600
Personal Allowance 2015/16	£(10,600)
Tax liability	NIL

---

36. 'Special Rate' Allowance

Special rules apply for the claiming of capital allowances on the purchase of 'integral features' that comprise the following are relevant to property lettings:

- solar heating;
- electrical system, including a lighting system;
- cold water system;
- heating system, a powered system of ventilation, air cooling or air purification, and any floor or ceiling in such a system;
- lift or escalator.

Any item not on this list, even if it forms part of the building, is outside the scope of the integral features rules.

Expenditure on such assets in excess of any claim under the Annual Investment Allowance (AIA) is allocated to a 'special rate' pool of 8% on a written down balance.

'Special Rate' Allowance

Diana spends a total of £14,000 on 'integral features' for her properties. The AIA limit has already been exceeded for the period and writing down allowances (WDA) need to be claimed.

The expenditure is allocated to the 'special rate' pool, the calculation being:

Additions:	
Electrical lighting system	£10,000
Air conditioning	£4,000
	£14,000
WDA at 8%	£(1,120)
Balance of allowances carried forward	£12,880
Total allowances claim	£1,120

37. Vehicles

If a van is used in the letting business to travel between properties or from office to property, the purchase cost of the van is allowed in full under the Annual Investment Allowance (AIA).

AIA is not available for a claim on cars; cars attract a writing down allowance (WDA) of 18% per annum, or 8% if the vehicle's CO_2 emissions exceed 130g/km. The allowance is 100% if it is a new car with CO_2 of 75g/km.

For capital allowances claims, the claim can only represent the proportion of business use of the asset – private use being disallowed.

However, if a car owned by a company is required to be garaged on company premises overnight with private use essentially being forbidden, then the whole WDA is allowed against the company's profits.

It is difficult to claim the full WDA successfully on a car owned by an individual because HMRC will normally argue that the car must be used privately to some extent.

Vehicles

David purchased a car a couple of years ago and in April 2015 started to use it in his business – the car's value is £5,000 with CO_2 emissions of 165g/km. He calculates that the car is used 75% of the time on business.

The WDA claim for 2015/16 is calculated as:

£5,000 x 8% x 75% = £300.

The amount carried forward to 2016/17 = £4,600 (i.e. £5,000 – £400, being the total WDA before restricting for private use).

38. Business Premises Renovation Allowance

The Business Premises Renovation Allowance (BPRA) allows 100% capital allowances to be claimed on the cost of conversion of derelict or unused business premises – dependent upon specific conditions being met.

One condition is that relief is only available for renovating or converting disused business premises in what is designated a 'disadvantaged area' (as specified in the Assisted Areas Order 2007).

If the full allowance is not claimed then a writing down allowance is available at 25% annually (25% of the initial qualifying expenditure) on a straight-line basis.

There is a 'balancing charge' adjustment if a specific 'balancing event' occurs within seven years, e.g. sale of property. The balancing charge will arise if proceeds received exceed the amount of allowance claimed.

BPRA ends on 31 March 2017 for companies and 5 April 2017 for other businesses.

Business Premises Renovation Allowance

Emily buys a derelict shop and renovates it, converting it into a cafe. The renovation costs £150,000 for which she makes a claim for 100% relief. After four years she sells the cafe for £200,000 – the sale is deemed a 'balancing event' as it occurs within seven years.

A 'balancing charge' arises. The residue on sale is nil as all of the allowance has been claimed. The proceeds of sale exceed the initial claim so the charge is capped at £150,000.

39.   Ancillary Expenses

When a property business undertakes expenditure that is capital in nature such that a capital allowance is claimed, then that cost can be augmented by 'ancillary' expenses.

Such ancillary expenses include labour and material expenses paid to install an item of plant or equipment plus costs of structural alterations to a building to accommodate the new plant.

Professional fees paid to architects or structural engineers can also be claimed provided it can be proved that the costs relate directly to the installation of the plant and machinery.

Ancillary Expenses

The availability of tax relief on ancillary expenses produces a tax planning possibility.

Tony bought a commercial building but after an inspection was advised to install a lift.

 A lift is eligible for capital allowances but the actual lift shaft is considered to be part of the building. If the lift had been installed at the time of building, the cost of the lift shaft would be ineligible for capital allowances and as such would not be relievable until the sale of the building as a capital gains tax cost.

However, as Tony has decided to install the lift *after* the building has been built the lift shaft becomes ancillary to the installation of qualifying machinery, is an ancillary cost and as such is allowable for capital allowances.

---

40.   Sale Of Commercial Property – s198 Election (1)

When a commercial property is sold, part of the selling price will include the value of fixtures that have qualified for capital allowances in the seller's business.

If the proceeds of sale on those assets exceed the written down value of the 'pool' there will be a 'balancing charge'. A 'balancing charge' is treated as a negative allowance whereby any capital allowances previously claimed will be clawed back.

It is mandatory for a formal 's198 election' to be made between the two parties, enabling agreement of a value for capital allowances purposes only, not exceeding the original purchase price of the assets. If the parties do not agree to this joint election, the purchaser (and any subsequent buyer) is prohibited from claiming any capital allowances on those fixtures.

The seller will want to set a value as low as possible to maximise allowances but the purchaser will want to agree a value that enables him or her to make some amount of claim carrying forward.

Sale Of Commercial Property – s198 Election (1)

Steve sells an industrial unit to Fred. He originally purchased it in 2007 for £250,000 and the agreed price is £300,000.

Steve has previously claimed capital allowances on air conditioning and security systems costing £50,000.

If the written down value of the assets at the point of Steve's sale to Fred was £20,000 and with the corresponding proceeds value restricted to Steve's original cost of £50,000, £30,000 allowances that Steve has previously claimed will be 'clawed' back.

If the value agreed under the election is £100, Steve will be able to claim a balancing allowance on sale of £19,900 but Fred will only be able to claim £100 going forward.

41. Sale Of Commercial Property – s198 Election (2)

The tax rules state that the purchaser's entitlement to capital allowances in relation to commercial property are restricted to the disposal value that the vendor of the property brought into account, even if this was not the immediate past owner.

Furthermore, it is the purchaser's responsibility to obtain and provide details of prior claims and disposal values, which might prove difficult if the original owner has ceased trading or if records are no longer available.

It is also a condition that the vendor must 'pool' the qualifying expenditure (i.e. add it to his or her own capital allowances computations). This includes expenditure incurred many years beforehand, which he or she may have neglected to claim thus far.

There are some categories of expenditure that the vendor may not have been able to claim when the costs were incurred – these may pass through to the purchaser without having been pooled, or be included in a joint 's198 election'. The most likely category is integral features installed before April 2008.

Sale Of Commercial Property – 's198 Election' (2)

In the tax case of *Mr and Mrs Tapsell and Mr Lester v HMRC* the partners purchased a care home as a going concern.

They made a claim for capital allowances totalling £146,014 – the figure being based on an apportionment of the purchase price. £106,014 of this amount related to the purchase of plant and machinery plus £40,000 that had been allocated as 'fixtures and fittings' in the contract.

Shortly afterwards, the sellers submitted a capital allowances claim of £68,811 for the same tax year. They provided no supporting details to HMRC, they then emigrated and could not be traced by either Mr and Mrs Tapsell or HMRC.

HMRC disallowed Mr and Mrs Tapsell's capital allowances claim on the grounds that they failed to show that the sellers had not previously claimed allowances on those fixtures.

Chapter 4.
Use Of Losses

42. Losses

Losses from a property business are calculated in the same way as losses from a trade.

Losses made on the same type of property are automatically offset against profits made on other properties in the same portfolio for the same period – being 'pooled' together.

Separate 'pools' are used for similar types of property, e.g. those not let on a commercial basis and foreign properties. Thus, two distinct and separate 'pools' will be created should there be both UK and foreign properties in a portfolio.

Losses on furnished holiday lettings (FHLs) are also kept separate and cannot be offset against either other UK rental profits or profits made on foreign properties.

Losses

Joan owns two properties – one in France and one in London.

She lets out both properties – the London one for the full year but the one in France for only two months over the summer. She makes a net profit on the property in London but a net loss on the one in France. Neither constitutes an FHL.

The loss on the French property cannot be offset against the profits made on the London property and must be kept separate.

However, the loss can be carried forward and deducted against any profit made on any future lettings of the French property or indeed, on any other overseas non-FHL properties Joan might subsequently acquire.

---

43. Losses Carried Forward

If there is an overall income tax loss made for a tax year, then unless the loss arises in relation to certain capital allowances, the loss is generally relieved as follows:

- Carried forward and set against profits made in future years on properties in the same UK property business (or if overseas property, against the same overseas property business).
- If the loss arises on or after cessation, relief may be set against the owners' general income or against capital gains made, in certain circumstances.
- Losses from UK furnished holiday lettings (FHLs) can only be carried forward and set against profits made on other UK FHL properties. When a property ceases to be an FHL, any unclaimed losses are wasted. Should the property be continued to be let, but as unfurnished, then the income and expenditure will be pooled with any other non-furnished lettings and taxed accordingly.

Losses Carried Forward

Ben owns a portfolio of four properties (none of which is a furnished holiday let). Together an overall loss was incurred for the year 2014/15 but a profit was made for the year 2015/16.

Ben's other income makes him a basic rate taxpayer.

Calculation:

2014/15 Loss carried forward	£(20,000)
2015/16 Profit	£10,000
Loss carried forward to 2016/17	£(10,000)

Nil tax due on lettings for either years 2014/15 or 2015/16.

44. Excess Capital Allowances Claim

If there is an overall income tax loss on an individual's (not a company's) continuing property portfolio over a tax year and that loss has been created by excess capital allowances claimed, then that loss can be relieved by being offset against the owner's other ('general') income for the same and/or next tax year. Otherwise the loss is automatically carried forward and set against future profits of the same UK property business.

The loss would best be used against other income for the same and/or next tax year if the taxpayer had taxable income in excess of the personal allowance.

If other income exceeds the personal allowance, better tax planning would be to carry forward the loss, so as not to waste the loss against income already covered by the personal allowance – remember also that capital allowances can be disclaimed (restricted) to suit. The loss can be set against the current year, or the following year, or both if large enough. Any unutilised loss is carried forward for offset against future rental profits.

Excess Capital Allowances Claim

James owns a portfolio of four properties. He purchased capital assets and claimed Annual Investment Allowance producing an overall loss of £10,000.

 If he is a taxpayer with income in excess of the personal allowance he can claim for the loss to be offset, thereby reducing his taxable income resulting in a possible tax refund.

If he has no other income the loss should be carried forward and offset against profits of the future period, if any.

101 Property Tax Secrets Revealed

45.   Loss Relief 'Cap'

Taxpayers seeking to obtain in excess of £50,000 of otherwise unlimited income tax reliefs in any one year are restricted in their claim to the higher of:

- 25% of their total income, or
- £50,000.

One of the tax reliefs is property tax loss relief, which is available for offset against total income – most commonly where some or all of the loss is attributable to capital allowances. The restriction does not apply to property loan interest as that is deemed an expense.

The 'capped' loss will not be wasted as it can be relieved by offset against the owner's other ('general') income in the next tax year, with any 'uncapped' amount being carried forward and set against future profits of the same UK property business.

Loss Relief 'Cap'

Mark has total income of £300,000 for 2015/16. He has made pension contributions of £30,000 gross, has paid £50,000 in (non-property related) loan interest and has a property loss eligible for sideways relief of £30,000.

The amount of 'uncapped reliefs' equals £80,000, exceeding the 'cap' 'de minimis' of £50,000. The total 'uncapped' relief thus available for offset is calculated as 25% x (£300,000 – £30,000 pension) = £67,500.

It would be preferable for the loan interest to be claimed in full with £17,500 of property loss; the remainder being carried forward and available for offset against the 2016/17 total income.

66   www.taxinsider.co.uk

46.   Dormant Periods

Losses from a rental business can only be set against future profits if the business is a continuing business.

In some instances it will not be clear as to whether a property business has ceased as the rental activities may stop and then restart. HMRC apply a general ruling by which they regard the 'old' business as ceasing if there is a gap of at least three years between lets and different properties are let in the taxpayer's old and new letting activities.

Thus, a business is not normally treated as having ceased simply because the property is not let for a period to allow for repairs or renovations.

However, the property business may be treated as having ceased and then recommencing should the property be used as the taxpayer's main residence between lets.

The losses of a ceased property business cannot be set against the profits of a 'new' property business.

47. Cessation Of Business

Where a non-corporate property business ceases, a post-cessation relief allowing offset against current income may be available. The claim is possible where, within seven years of the business ceasing, the taxpayer is required to make a 'qualifying payment', or a 'qualifying event' has occurred in connection with the ceased business.

- 'Qualifying payments' include the remedying of defective work and legal expenses in connection with such defects, or expenses incurred in collecting outstanding business debts.
- 'Qualifying events' arise when debts taken into account in calculating the profits or losses of the business subsequently prove to be bad, or are released, after cessation.

The maximum must be offset against income first and then the balance may be relieved against any capital gains accruing in the same year.

Cessation Of Business

Dawn sold the last property in her portfolio on 25 July 2008.

In January 2015 she loses a court case for defective services and is obliged to make a compensation payment of £10,000.

Her P60 for 2014/15 shows taxable income of £30,000.

If she makes a claim by 31 January 2017 she can offset the £10,000 against her 2014/15 income and obtain a tax refund.

48.   Capital Losses – Negligible Value

Tax relief is available when an asset is lost, destroyed or becomes of negligible value – this is possible, for example, when a Buy To Let property is purchased 'off plan', the builder goes into liquidation, money is lost and the property is never built.

To claim the relief:

- The investor must still own the property when it becomes of negligible value.
- The amount of relief is calculated as if the property had been sold and immediately reacquired.
- The claim can be made for an earlier time in the previous two tax years in which the deemed disposal occurred (see example) or for companies, any accounting period ending not more than two years before the date of the claim. This allows the claim to be backdated to a year when the loss can be most profitably used. For the claim to be allowed it may be necessary to demonstrate to HMRC that the asset had already become of negligible value, at that earlier time.
- The claim is not automatic and needs to be made on the Tax Return.

Capital Losses – Negligible Value

In November 2014 Fred entered into an agreement with a developer to buy a flat 'off plan' for £200,000. A deposit of 10% was paid plus legal fees of £3,500.

In January 2015 Fred received a letter informing him that the developer had gone into liquidation.

A year later, in January 2016, it is confirmed that the development will not be going ahead and therefore Fred will not be receiving repayment of the deposit.

The loss of £(43,500) ((£200,000 x 2 x 10%) + £3,500) is treated as a normal capital loss for either offset against other gains made during the same year of claim or carried forward against future gains.

The offset could apply for the tax year as early as 2015/16 on the basis that that was the year in which the money was 'lost'.

49. Capital Losses – Negligible Value – Spouse/Civil Partners

Tax planning possibility:

- Disposals between spouses/civil partners are deemed to occur on a 'no gain/no loss' basis.
- If one spouse/civil partner owns an asset which, on sale, has produced a capital gain in excess of the annual exempt amount and the other spouse/civil partner has an asset standing at a potential negligible-value loss, the negligible value asset can be transferred to the spouse/civil partner, the loss offset and capital gain reduced.

Capital Losses – Negligible Value – Spouse/Civil Partners

Continued from Tip 48.

As at 1 January 2016 the flat stands at a negligible-value asset loss of £43,500 but in February 2016 Fred's wife sells a property owned in her own name which produces a chargeable capital gain of £60,000.

If Fred were to transfer the loss-making asset to his wife by 5 April 2016, the end of the tax year, she could offset the loss against the gains made and receive a reduced capital gains tax bill.

Chapter 5.
Foreign Matters

50.   Non-Resident Landlord Scheme

The 'Non-Resident Landlord Scheme' (NRLS) is a scheme for taxing the UK rental income of non-resident landlords. Usually basic rate tax is deducted from the net rent collected by an agent (less expenses paid) or paid by a tenant unless the agent/tenant has authority from HMRC to pay the landlord gross.

'Non-resident landlords' under this scheme are persons (individuals, companies, trustees) who are in receipt of UK rental income, and whose 'usual place of abode' is outside of the UK.

Although the scheme refers to 'non-resident' landlords, it is the 'usual place of abode' and not residency that determines whether a landlord is within the scheme or not.

An absence from the UK of six months or more determines that a person has a 'usual place of abode' outside of the UK. It is therefore possible for a person to be tax resident in the UK yet, for the purposes of the scheme, to have a 'usual place of abode' outside of the UK.

Rent can be paid gross on application using Form NRL1. HMRC will formally approve the application where satisfied that the applicant's UK tax affairs are up-to-date or that the rental income will be non-taxable (e.g. where covered by personal allowances).

On receipt of the 'Notice of Approval' tax will not be withheld and a tenant will not be required to make any returns post the date of approval. An agent will have to submit an annual return but will not be required to submit the usual quarterly returns.

51. NRLS – Agents

The 'Non-Resident Landlord Scheme' (NRLS) requires persons who act as 'representatives' (agents) for the landlord to deduct basic rate tax from the net rent collected (less expenses paid) unless the agent has authority from HMRC to pay the landlord gross.

The tax is paid on a quarterly basis and an information return is submitted. An annual return must also be submitted by 5 July after each tax year-end and a certificate issued to the landlord confirming tax paid.

NRLS – Agents

John has been working abroad for eight months and rents out his UK property via a letting agent. The letting agent pays all expenses on his behalf, deducting them from the rent received.

The property is let at £800 per month and the expenses are £250.

The amount of net rental profit John will receive is calculated as being:

£(800 – 250) x 80% = £440

The tax bill is £110 per month (i.e. £(800 – 250) x 20%).

52.   NRLS – Non-Agent

The 'Non-Resident Landlords Scheme' (NRLS) requires that where there is no UK-based representative/agent, the rent being paid directly to a landlord who lives outside of the UK, the tenant must deduct basic rate tax from the rent paid and pay the tax to HMRC on a quarterly basis.

- The calculation is of tax on the gross amount actually payable to the landlord (plus any payments made by the tenant where the payment is not a deductible expense).
- Tenants do not have to operate the scheme if the rent paid is less than £5,200 per annum.
- Where the tenant occupies the property for only part of the year the threshold of £5,200 is proportionately reduced.
- Where two or more people share a property as tenants the £5,200 limit applies separately to each in respect of each share of the rent.
- The tenant must make the tax payment plus submit an information return to HMRC confirming tax paid on a quarterly basis within 30 days of the end of each quarter (30 June, 30 September, 31 December and 31 March).
- By 5 July after the tax year-end, the tenant must submit an annual return to HMRC and a certificate to the landlord confirming payments made.

Further details of the scheme can be found at:
https://www.gov.uk/tax-uk-income-live-abroad/rent.

53.   NRLS – Excess Expenses

Under the 'Non-Resident Landlord Scheme' (NRLS) where the deductible expenses exceed rental income for any quarter the excess expenses are:

- carried back for offset against rental income paid to the same landlord for previous quarters in the same tax year, on a 'last in, first out' basis; then
- carried forward for offset against future quarters' net rental profits.

Repayments

Carry back will result in a repayment of tax for the previous quarter in the tax year – the amount can be deducted from any tax due for other NRLS lettings of the current quarter.

Should it not be possible to deduct the refund because it relates to a previous tax year, a claim to HMRC is required.

NRLS – Excess Expenses

John has been working abroad for nine months and rents out his UK property via a letting agent. The letting agent pays all the expenses on his behalf, deducting them from the rent received.

The property is let at £800 per quarter. The expenses for the quarter to 31 March 2015 were £1,000 and for the quarter to 30 June 2015 were £1,400.

Tax year 2014/15
Quarter to 30 December 2014
Profit	£800
Tax	£160

Quarter to 31 March 2015
Rent	£800
Less expenses	£(1,000)
Carry back loss to previous quarter	£(200)
Tax refund £200 @ 20%	£40

Tax year 2015/16
Quarter to 30 June 2015
Rent	£800
Less expenses	£(1,400)
Excess expenses	£(600)

The £(600) excess cannot be carried back to the previous quarter, as the quarter is not in the same tax year. Rather, it will be carried forward to be offset against future net profit (if the property remains rented). If the property ceases to be rented the excess cannot be used by the agent.

NOTE: The biggest expense is likely to be mortgage interest, which is not paid by the agent and therefore cannot be offset. Hence many NRLS landlords have to wait until the year-end to claim any refund due via submission of a Tax Return.

54.   Non-Resident Companies

The 'Annual Tax on Enveloped Dwellings' (ATED) was introduced in 2013 to tackle the avoidance of stamp duty land tax. The charge relates to residential property with a value over £1m owned by a 'non-natural person', generally a company or a partnership with a corporate member. Properties valued in the £1m to £2m band are charged £7,000 per annum, and the bands increase such that properties valued at over £20m are charged £218,200. From 1 April 2016 a further band will come into effect for properties with a value greater than £500,000 but not more than £1m, attracting an annual charge of £3,500. The charge is paid in advance, annually and in the year of purchase plus there are in-year filing requirements.

Although this tax is aimed at the foreign wealthy property investor, it will also affect all British Nationals temporarily living abroad and those emigrating and retiring abroad, as many use the facility of placing property within corporate 'envelopes'. However, this approach may still be beneficial for taxpayers wishing to save IHT.

Chapter 6.
Selling Property

55. Capital Gains Tax

Capital gains tax (CGT) is charged on the net gains (proceeds less cost) made on the sale of assets by individuals, personal representatives and trustees. Companies do not pay CGT but they are charged to corporation tax on net gains made.

Charge to CGT

A UK resident and domiciled property investor is liable to CGT where:

- a property is sold at a higher price than the original purchase price wherever situated in the world, or
- a property or part of a property is transferred to an individual who is not the transferor's spouse/civil partner.

UK resident but non-domiciled persons are liable to CGT on UK assets and on gains brought into the country (known as the 'remittance basis').

Calculation of the tax

- Gains (or losses) are calculated separately for each asset.
- The net gains/losses for each property sold in a tax year are totalled and if the overall gain exceeds the annual exempt amount (£11,100 for individuals in 2015/16 and 2016/17), the balance is taxed at the taxpayer's highest rate of tax applicable to capital gains (i.e. for individuals at 18% for any amount falling within the basic rate band and 28% for any surplus).
- A disposal may give rise to a gain or loss.
- The most common and valuable exemption is the main Principal Private Residence exemption (see Chapter 7).

56. Consideration – 'Arm's Length' Rule

A property deal is termed as being made at 'arm's length' if it is a normal commercial transaction between two or more persons. A transaction not likely to be at arm's length is one undertaken by persons related by blood, adoption or marriage, or who are living together.

HMRC requires a valuation of property if the transaction has not been made at 'arm's length'. The valuation will determine the market value and that is the figure that will be used as the proceeds amount in the capital gains tax (CGT) calculation on sale or other disposal.

Consideration – 'Arm's Length' Rule

Anton needs to sell his property quickly so that he can move abroad. Tony is aware that Anton needs a quick sale and therefore offers him a low price. No one else has made an offer. Anton accepts the offer.

The price was not the best possible price that could have achieved if the property had been left on the market for longer but Anton was trying to achieve the best deal possible in the time allowed.

This is deemed to be a bad bargain rather than being a bargain not made at 'arm's length' and therefore the proceeds received will be used in any CGT calculation.

If Anton and Tony had been related (i.e. 'connected persons') HMRC would require a market valuation.

57. Valuing Land

A capital gains tax (CGT) charge may arise on the disposal of land. In order to calculate the capital gain or loss arising, a valuation is required where:

- The land was owned at 31 March 1982 (in order to determine the 'base cost' of the property).
- The disposal was a bargain not at 'arm's length'.
- The disposal was to a connected person.
- There is a part disposal of the land and the usual part disposal basis is applied, which requires a valuation of the retained part.
- There has already been a part disposal and the 'alternative basis' of calculation has not been used.

Calculation

- Valuation – professional advice is required.
- 'Alternative' basis – the land disposed of is treated as a separate asset – HMRC will accept any 'reasonable and fair' method of apportionment of the base cost.

Valuing Land

Where a CGT computation requires a valuation HMRC offer a free valuation check. This service is available only after the disposal has been made but before completion of the Tax Return, so you cannot ask for a check in advance of sale. Should HMRC's valuation differ from the taxpayer's valuation, HMRC give alternatives and reasons.

58.   Surrender Premiums

A premium is a sum paid by a tenant to a landlord either on the creation or surrender of an interest in a property.

Surrender premiums payable to terminate a lease early are generally tax inefficient; depending on the length of the lease and whether or not there is a provision in the agreement for early termination, the landlord will be taxed on a capital and/or revenue receipt whilst the tenant receives neither a capital nor revenue deduction.

Tax planning possibilities:

- Rather than pay the premium the tenant incentivises a third party (the new tenant) to accept assignment of the lease. The payment is tax free in the new tenant's hands and they may be willing to accept a lower incentive from the existing tenant as a share of the tax saving from which he or she will benefit. The agreement must be made directly between the existing and new tenant without any input from the landlord.

- The tenant offers the landlord a sum representing the future rent due with an appropriate discount to represent the cash-flow benefit to the landlord. The tenant then sub-lets to the landlord for the remainder of the lease period at a peppercorn rent, thus enabling the landlord to not lose out financially compared with an outright surrender. The tenant will be able to claim a tax deduction for the sum paid and if that amount is close to the original premium, the tax relief improves the tenant's position. The landlord would have to consider his or her position as the receipt will be of income and not capital.

59.   Entrepreneurs' Relief

Only individuals can claim Entrepreneurs' Relief; it cannot be claimed by companies. There is a lifetime limit for the claim of £10m. The effect of the relief is to reduce the capital gains tax rate charge from 28% or 18% to 10%.

The relief extends to disposals made within 36 months of cessation of trading, provided that the business qualified for the 12 months up to the cessation of the business.

In order that the disposal of shares in a company is eligible for the relief, certain conditions need to be met including that the individual shareholder must have held at least 5% of the ordinary share capital and voting rights.

Only 5% of the shares need to be held for at least 12 months, which creates a planning opportunity. If a spouse does not work in a company, 12 months before the planned sale date he or she can be appointed a director or company secretary with a 5% share. Once this test has been satisfied more shares can be transferred to the spouse shortly before a sale and the gain still qualifies for relief.

Entrepreneurs' Relief is only available on a capital gain arising on the disposal of a business asset that is linked to, or takes place as part of, a disposal of all or part of a business. For these purposes a 'business' is a trade, profession or vocation.

Thus, the relief is not generally available on disposals of residential property held as an investment, but is allowed on the sale of furnished holiday lets (as these properties are regarded as business assets).

Relief is also potentially available on the disposal of a property that has been used as a main residence and a business, in which case the property should be sold no later than 18 months after the sale of the business to ensure that the Principal Private Residence Relief can be claimed.

Entrepreneurs' Relief

Mr Jones, a dentist, runs his practice from a surgery attached to his home, which is calculated as 25% of the property area.

He is disposing of his home and business on retirement.

The gain on the property disposal is £800,000 and the goodwill is £400,000.

The tax liability for 2015/16 will be:

Gain on home 25% x £800,000	£200,000
Gain on Goodwill	£400,000
Total Gain	£600,000
Less Annual Exemption 2015/16	£(11,100)
Chargeable Gain	£588,900
Tax liability @ 10%	£58,890

Chapter 7.
Main Residence Relief

60. Conditions

When an individual sells his only or main residence, generally the gain is exempt from capital gains tax due to Principal Private Residence (PPR) relief. The conditions are that the property must:

1. not have been purchased 'wholly or partly' for the reason of making a gain; and
2. be the individual's only or main residence at some point of ownership or claimed to be so.
3. From 6 April 2015 the main residence will only be eligible for PPR if the owner was resident in the UK for the tax year or has spent at least 90 midnights in the property.

The last 18 months ownership of a property that has been the individual's only or main residence at some time of ownership is always treated as occupation for the purposes of this relief, regardless of whether the taxpayer is actually resident during those last 18 months. In recognition that a person who is disabled (or their spouse/civil partner) or going into a care home may take longer to sell the residence, the last 36 months are exempt.

Conditions

Joan bought Rose Cottage on 1 June 2000, living there continuously until she inherited Brook House on 1 January 2003. She stayed at Brook House during the week as it was more convenient for her job, using Rose Cottage as a weekend retreat. Joan sold Rose Cottage on 1 June 2015.

Without a PPR election, Rose Cottage would be classed as Joan's PPR from 1 June 2000 to 31 December 2002 PLUS she would be allowed the 18 months from 2 December 2012 to the date of sale on 1 June 2015. Rose Cottage would not qualify for PPR relief for the period 1 January 2003 to 1 December 2012.

61. 'Residence'

Legislation does not define exactly what constitutes a 'residence' but in the tax case of *Batey v Wakefield* (1981) it was decided that not only can the main residence comprise more than one building but it can also include ancillary buildings that are used as houses in their own right (e.g. summerhouse, staff bungalow).

In the subsequent case of *Williams v Merrylees* (1987) the judge went further stating that *'what one is looking for is an entity which can be sensibly described as being a dwelling-house though split up into different buildings performing different functions'.*

Residence – Williams v Merrylees (1987)

A taxpayer purchased a small estate including a lodge sited approximately 200 metres from the main house. The lodge was occupied by a married couple who worked on the estate. The taxpayer sold the main house but retained the lodge after he moved.

When the occupants of the lodge died the taxpayer sold the lodge to the purchasers of the main house.

The commissioners found that the lodge was in the area of the main house and allowed the PPR relief claim.

62.   Proving PPR Status (1)

When deciding whether a property should be given Principal Private Residence (PPR) status HMRC look as to whether the owner had any *intention* of living in the property. It is a matter of fact whether a property is the PPR or not but to allow a PPR claim HMRC require proof that the property has actually been lived in as the PPR.

In *Metcalf v HMRC* (2010), lack of both oral and other evidence, including lack of consumption of electricity helped the Tribunal find in favour of HMRC.

Proving PPR Status (1) – Metcalfe v HMRC (2010)

Mr Metcalfe owned several properties but claimed one property as his PPR. The property was purchased 'off plan' and came with various fixtures and fittings (carpets, fridge, cooker, etc.).

As proof of non-permanence HMRC stated that no telephone had been installed but Mr Metcalfe argued that he always used his mobile; additional proof was required.

HMRC particularly cited the electricity bill showing low usage over the winter period suggesting non-residence. Mr Metcalfe argued that the bill was low because the apartment was new, had full double-glazing and he worked long shifts.

He insisted that he had purchased the property with the intention of living there permanently but his work took him elsewhere. The Tribunal found that Mr Metcalfe had lived there for a time but could find no proof of *'permanence, continuity and expectation of continuity of occupation'* (*Goodwin v Curtis* (1988)) as the evidence was flimsy and more concrete evidence was lacking.

63.   Proving PPR Status (2)

As well as there being the *'intention'* to occupy there must be a degree of permanence in order for Principal Private Residence (PPR) relief to be allowed, as cited in the tax case of *Piers Moore v HMRC* (2013).

Proving PPR Status (2) – Moore v HMRC (2013)

In this case evidence was submitted which the judge said proved occupancy but HMRC's case was again that the occupation did not have the necessary degree of *'permanence, continuity or expectation of continuity'* necessary for the claim to succeed.

The taxpayer remained in the property after his marriage had broken up and for some months before it was marketed. Indeed, the purchase of a new property with his new family was initiated six months after he had moved in.

Even so the Tribunal found for HMRC in that the property was temporary accommodation and not a permanent residence.

64.   Non-Residents And Main Residence Relief

Prior to 6 April 2015 where a person was non-resident no capital gains tax was charged on the disposal of a UK residential property. If the gain was not taxed in the country of residence then the gain would not be taxed at all. In comparison, UK residents who sold a property (wherever sited in the world) which was not their main residence would be subjected to capital gains tax.

From 6 April 2015, non-residents investing in UK residential property and UK residents investing in non-UK property will have to satisfy a 'day count test' in relation to that property. Now an individual will be eligible for Principal Private Residence (PPR) relief only if he or she was tax resident in the same country as the property for the relevant tax year or, if non-resident, that he or she spent at least 90 midnights in the property, or in other properties in the same country in the tax year. Spouses and civil partners can only have one residence between them and residence by one spouse/civil partner will be deemed to the residence of the other.

Non-residents will be able to nominate that a UK property meeting the 90-day rule is their main residence for a tax year at the time of sale.

The rules mean that individuals who are resident in the UK will remain eligible for PPR but non-residents will need to meet the 90-day rule. UK residents who have overseas property will also need to satisfy the 90-day rule even if they have already elected for the second home overseas to be their main residence for PPR.

Individuals who retire abroad but keep their homes in the UK, will be entitled to PPR for the years they were in the UK, but will be subject to the 90-day rule thereafter for each tax year (apart from the last 18 months of ownership).

Gains attributed to periods before 6 April 2015 will not be subject to the new charge. The non-UK resident is able to 'rebase' the property to 6 April 2015 market value or, if more beneficial, can either time-apportion the gain or have the entire gain/loss taken into account.

Non-Residents And Main Residence Relief

Julienne is resident in France and owns a flat in London. In 2015/16 she stayed 80 midnights. Her husband John accompanies her on 30 of those nights. He stayed on for an extra 12 midnights on business. Julienne passes the 90 'midnights test' because the property has been occupied by one of them for 92 midnights.

If John stays on for only nine extra midnights the test will fail because the property will have been occupied for only 89 midnights.

---

65. 'Flipping'

As long as the initial election for Principal Private Residence (PPR) relief has been made, it can then be varied ('flipped') as many times as desired by submitting a further election. There is no prescribed form or wording for the election but it must be made within two years of a change in *'combination of residences'*. Should the two-year time limit be missed, there needs to be a 'trigger' event in order to reset the election date.

Examples of 'trigger' events that could be used to change the *'combination of residences'* are:

- Marriage/civil partnership – both parties owning property used as their respective residence, or where there is joint ownership. Married couples/civil partners can only have one main residence qualifying for PPR such that any election made must be made jointly.
- Renting out one of the properties – when the letting comes to an end the owner can then take up residence.
- Selling half of one residence such that the seller is no longer in full ownership but is still in residence.
- Transferring ownership of a main residence into a trust under which the owner has a beneficial interest, with the proviso that the owner remains in residence. Care is needed so as not to be caught under the 'gift with reservation of benefit' or 'pre-owned asset' rules.

PPR is a valuable tax relief and 'flipping' is legitimate tax planning. However, if used too many times or in quick succession, there is the danger that HMRC will investigate in an attempt to prove that either the PPR exemption is invalid and that the real reason for nominating the properties is avoidance of tax or that the owner should be taxed under the income tax rather than capital gains tax rules as a 'serial seller'.

'Flipping'
John's main residence is in Woking; his father lives in Camberley. John's father dies and leaves his house to John, who lives in it at weekends.
John is unaware of the election required and misses the election date. Three years after his father's death the election has still not been made.
John marries Jane and the property is transferred into joint ownership. On marriage the election can be made.

66.   Delay In Occupation

There is a limited concession to extend Principal Private Residence (PPR) relief should the owner not move into his or her only or main residence on purchase. This covers situations where the owner:

- buys land on which the house is to be built;
- has the house altered or redecorated before moving in;
- remains in the first property whilst it is still on the market, provided that when that property is sold the second property becomes the owner's only or main residence.

In these circumstances, the period before occupation is allowed as PPR providing that the period between acquisition and actual occupation is 12 months or less. This period may be extended to a maximum of two years, but only if HMRC is satisfied there is a good reason for the delay in occupation.

If the effect of this relief means that the owner temporarily has two PPR properties, an election is not required.

Delay In Occupation

Jim purchased 1 Back Lane on 1 January 1990 as his PPR. On 1 June 2013 he purchased 1 Front Lane intending to live there and rent Back Lane.

Unfortunately whilst undertaking some building work he discovered that Front Lane was deemed unsafe and returned to live in Back Lane whilst the repair work was being undertaken. The building work took 18 months; Jim then moved into Front Lane which was eventually sold on 1 June 2015.

PPR is granted for the full period of ownership.

---

67. Deemed Occupation

There may be times when the owner is prevented from living in his or her main residence for reasons that are not the owner's by choice. It would be unfair for him or her not to be eligible for Principal Private Residence (PPR) relief for that period of absence.

'Deemed' occupation is only possible where the taxpayer is absent from the property and has no other residence eligible for PPR.

There is no minimum period of occupation for PPR relief but usually the house has to be physically occupied as a residence before and after any period of absence. Should the reason for the absence be that the owner was working away, then he or she does not have to return to the house if work subsequently requires residence elsewhere.

Absences can be cumulative as long as one of three conditions applies:

1. any period of absence – maximum three years, or
2. overseas employment (not self-employment) of the owner or spouse/civil partner – unlimited period, or
3. employment elsewhere (employed or self-employed) of the owner or spouse/civil partner – maximum four years.

Deemed Occupation

Stephen has a PPR property in Surrey but has worked in Wales for six years. His mother lives in Scotland and has recently become ill. Stephen intends to take unpaid leave from his job and be her carer.

He can do so for just one year to retain PPR on his Surrey property under the 'deemed occupation' rules.

His six years working in Wales have used:

- Condition 3) – four years – employment elsewhere in the UK.
- Condition 1) – two years – any period.
- One year remains under condition 1).

68. Conversion Of Property

Should a property that was initially a main residence be converted into flats and sold, Principal Private Residence (PPR) relief will be denied in respect of the gain attributable to the period of ownership whilst the conversion is taking place as the expenditure has been incurred *'wholly or partly'* for the purposes of realising a gain.

For the calculation a valuation of the property as not converted is required and then that figure is compared with the sale price post conversion in order to establish the additional profit attributable to the conversion.

Conversion Of Property

Tony lived in a property as his main residence from the date of purchase in July 1996 (cost = £100,000) to July 2012 when work commenced on conversion into three flats. Work was completed in December 2012, the flats finally all being sold in June 2015 for £250,000 each.

The conversion cost was £150,000. If the property had remained as one house the sale proceeds would have been £550,000.

The additional expenditure for conversion generated an additional gain of £50,000 calculated as follows:

	Total Gain	Exempt PPR Gain	Taxable Gain
Proceeds/valuation	£750,000	£550,000	£200,000
Original cost of property	£(100,000)	£(100,000)	
Conversion expenditure	£(150,000)		£(150,000)
Gain	£500,000	£450,000	£50,000

Less annual exemption, if available.

69.   PPR And Dependent Relative Relief

Principal Private Residence (PPR) relief is not allowed on the sale of property purchased as the residence of an elderly or infirm ('dependent') relative.

'Dependent relative' is defined as being the owner's own or their spouse/civil partner's widowed or separated mother or any other relative who is unable to look after themselves. PPR is allowed on property used by the relative pre 5 April 1988, providing that the relative was the property's sole resident, living there rent-free and continuing to do so until three years before sale.

Should there have been a change of occupant after 5 April 1988 the exemption is not allowed for the period after the change to the date of sale, even if the new occupant is another dependent relative.

PPR And Dependent Relative Relief

David acquired a property on 1 June 1986, selling it on 1 December 2015 realising a gain of £250,000. The house was provided rent-free and without any other consideration as the sole residence of David's widowed mother from 1 June 1986 to 1 December 1990 when she died. David's elderly mother-in-law then took up residence.

1 June 1986 – 1 December 2015   = 354 months

Sole residence of dependent relative:
1 June 1986 – 1 December 1990   = 54 months

Final period (last 18 months exempt)   = 18 months

PPR relief allowed:

$$\frac{54 \text{ months} + 18 \text{ months}}{354 \text{ months}} \times £250,000 \quad = £50,847$$

Chargeable gain: £250,000 less PPR of £50,847 = £199,153.

Less annual exemption, if available.

70.   Job-Related Accommodation

Where a taxpayer owns a property as his or her main residence but is obliged to live elsewhere in job-related accommodation, the property could be deemed not eligible for Principal Private Residence (PPR) relief. However, the relief will apply when, during the period of ownership the taxpayer:

- resides in other job-related accommodation; and
- intends to occupy the first property as his or her only or main residence at some time.

This 'job-related' provision is only possible if it is necessary or customary for the employee to live in accommodation provided by the employer for the better performance of their duties – it must not simply be a matter of choice.

The relief is allowed even if the first property is not occupied due to a change of circumstances, provided it has been the *intention* to occupy the property.

Job-Related Accommodation

Susan occupied her main residence until 2000 when her work required her to move into qualifying job-related accommodation in Scotland.

In 2005 she was sent to work in the Devon office but occupied privately rented accommodation. She purchased that property in 2007.

In 2015 the original residence was sold, not having been re-occupied. Until 2007 she had intended to return to her main residence.

PPR relief is allowed:

1. until 2000 before the move to Scotland;

2. for the period of job-related accommodation between 2000 to 2005;

3. for 2005 to 2007 as a permitted period of absence; and

4. for the final 18 months.

71.   'Permitted Area'

There is a restriction on the size of garden or grounds attached to a main residence that can be granted Principal Private Residence (PPR) relief.

The 'permitted area' must not exceed half a hectare (approximately 1.25 acres); this area is the total area, including the grounds on which the residence is built. However, a larger area may be permitted should it prove to be needed for the 'reasonable enjoyment' of the house as a residence, commensurate with the size and character of the property.

Care must be taken as to the order of sale – if the property is sold before the land then capital gains tax (CGT) will be charged as the land will no longer be 'attached' to the residence.

If land in grounds larger than half a hectare is sold before the property and PPR is claimed, HMRC will want to know what has changed such that land necessary for the 'reasonable enjoyment' of the house before sale was not so required afterwards.

'Permitted Area' – Varty v Lynes (1976)

Mr Varty purchased a house comprising land of less than one acre. He sold the house with part of the garden and applied for planning permission for the remainder which was sold four years later.

HMRC charged CGT on the second sale and the taxpayer appealed, contending that the land had been 'enjoyed' as part of his main residence and that the gain was PPR exempt.

It was held that PPR did not apply.

72. Working From Home

Principal Private Residence relief cannot be claimed for any part of the main residence that is used exclusively for business use.

To protect the exemption, any part of the home that is used for business purposes needs to also be available for private use. For example, a room used as an office from which to run the business during the day could also be used by the taxpayer's children to do their homework in the evening.

Where there is exclusive business use, any gain arising on sale must be apportioned and the proportion relating to exclusive business use will be charged to capital gains tax (CGT). However, the gain relating to the use of one room may be below the annual exempt amount and not be charged.

Working From Home

Julia runs a marketing business from home. Her home has eight rooms and she uses one exclusively as an office.

On the sale of her property, she realises a gain of £50,000.

One-eighth (£6,250) would be charged to CGT.

To the extent that her annual exemption (£11,100 for the tax year 2015/16) remains available, this would shelter the gain with the result that no CGT is payable.

73.   Lettings Relief

A property that is rented qualifies for 'residential lettings exemption' ('Lettings Relief') on sale but only if the residence has been the owner's main residence (or elected to be so) at any time during the period of ownership.

The exemption is restricted to the smallest of £40,000, the amount attributable to the period for which the property was let or the amount equal to the exempt gain on the proportion of the property that is deemed to be the Principal Private Residence. The relief is per person; therefore a property owned jointly is allowed maximum relief of £80,000.

It has not been confirmed via any court case but there seems to be no reason why a property let under the 'furnished holiday lettings' rules should not be eligible to claim 'Lettings Relief', provided that the property has been the owner's main residence at some time during the period of ownership.

Lettings Relief

Holly bought a property eight years ago for £200,000 and lived in it for a year before letting it out for seven years. The property was sold for £296,000 giving a gain of £96,000 before Lettings Relief and Principal Private Residence (PPR) relief.

Lettings Relief will be the lower of:

- £40,000

- £30,000 (amount of PPR – 2.5*/8 x £96,000), and

- £84,000 (gain attributable to letting – 7/8 x £96,000).

  * 12 months of residence plus last 18 months = 2.5 years.

Chapter 8.
Gifting Property

74. Gift Between Spouses/Civil Partners

If a gift of a property (or share of a property) is made or a property is sold at less than its market value, capital gains tax (CGT) is charged as if the donor had received the market value in cash.

This ruling does not apply to transfers (gifts) between spouses/civil partnerships. In this situation the donee is treated as having acquired the property at the date of the transaction, but most importantly at the original purchase price.

No CGT will be due until the receiving spouse/civil partner sells the property.

Gift Between Spouses/Civil Partners

Joe is a 45% additional rate taxpayer who owns a Buy To Let property originally purchased for £150,000. He gifts the property to his son on 1 July 2015 when its value is £250,000.

Joe is deemed to have received the market value and as such his CGT tax liability is:

Market value less original price	£100,000
Less Annual Exemption 2015/16	£(11,100)
Chargeable Gain	£88,900
Tax due @ 28%	£24,892

However, there will be a practical problem in that no monies will have been received out of which to pay the CGT.

If Joe had gifted the property to his wife no CGT would be due on transfer, but should his wife subsequently sell the property, the base value would be the original cost of £150,000.

---

75.   Gift Of PPR To Spouse/Civil Partner

Where there is an inter-spouse/civil partner transfer of a Principal Private Residence (PPR), the donee is still treated as having acquired the property at the donor's base cost but with one added twist – the donee's period of ownership is deemed to commence not at the date of transfer but instead at the date of the original acquisition by the donor.

Furthermore, any period during which the property was the main residence of the donor will also be deemed to be that of the donee such that the transaction is backdated.

This is only relevant to properties that are (or have been nominated as) the main Principal Private Residence.

Gift Of PPR To Spouse/Civil Partners

Joe purchases property 1 in his sole name as a main residence. A few years later he marries Jane, moves into property 2 and lets out property 1. Ten years later there is a large capital gain accruing on property 1.

Joe then transfers property 1 to Jane on a 'no gain/no loss' basis and they start also to occupy property 1 as a residence.

Joe and Jane elect property 1 as the main PPR. A few weeks later a further election is made back to property 2. Over the next few months Joe and Jane live in property 1 as a residence before the property is sold.

Under this specific ruling property 1 is deemed to be the main PPR for the period from the date of purchase to the date of transfer; then as the property has been a residence, the period between the date of transfer and the date of sale is also capital gains tax-free as it is covered by the 18-month rule.

76. Transfer Of Assets On Separation

The capital gains tax rules on gifts between spouses as being at 'no gain/no loss' apply until the end of the tax year of separation. Ideally therefore, the transfer of any jointly held assets should be made some time before the end of the tax year in which separation took place in order to be fully exempt. The asset (which could include the main residence) will be valued as at the date of the gift rather than the 50% share of the original cost. Thus an 'uplift' in the value of the property is achieved which may be beneficial should the property subsequently be sold but the owner not be able to take advantage of the full Principal Private Residence relief.

Should the transfer take place after the end of the tax year in which separation occurs but before the granting of the Decree Absolute, then the parties are treated as 'connected parties'; as such the disposal is automatically treated as being at market value whatever the actual amount paid.

Where a main residence and another property are owned jointly, there will be tax advantages should the departing spouse leave the former matrimonial home on separation and go to live in the second property.

Appropriate transfers of both properties in the tax year of separation, together with an election by each that the property they are occupying is their main residence, should ensure that gains on both properties are exempt.

Transfer Of Assets On Separation

Adam and Eve separate in May 2015. They jointly own a Buy To Let property. Adam transfers the property to Eve in August 2015.

The property originally cost £200,000 with costs of acquisition being £2,500. Legal costs on transfer were £2,500.

Adam's deemed disposal proceeds are:

Cost (50% share)	£100,000
Acquisition costs (50% share)	£(1,250)
Legal costs	£(2,500)
Total deemed proceeds	£103,750

Eve's revised base cost will therefore be her share (£101,250) plus £103,750 = £205,000.

77.   Transfer Of PPR On Separation

On separation many couples decide that one party is to remain in the main residence and the other party is to leave, transferring their interest to the other rather than immediately selling the property. If the transfer is made during the year of separation then the Principal Private Residence (PPR) relief is not affected should the property be sold at a later date.

Should the sale be after the date of separation PPR is still available for both parties so long as the property is sold within 18 months after the date of separation and one spouse leaving the family home.

A capital gains tax (CGT) charge will be triggered by one joint owner's interest not being fully covered by PPR. This situation may arise when, as part of the divorce settlement, the wife is awarded use of the marital home under a 'Mesher order', until such time as the children have finished school, the property then being sold and the proceeds split between the two parties. A 'Mesher' order is a court order that postpones the sale of the marital home, the actual date of sale being dependent upon certain specified events.

The only situation where HMRC permit more than 18 months is where the property is transferred to the remaining spouse under a 'Mesher' order AND an election has not been made by the former spouse for another house to be deemed the PPR.

Of course, if the house is sold after the 18 months having not been transferred to the remaining spouse, then CGT will be due on the gain attributable to the spouse who moved out, but only in the proportion of gain made after the 18 months in relation to the total period of ownership or 31 March 1982, whichever is the later date.

78. Exchange Of Interests

If a gift of property is made to a non-spouse/civil partner, capital gains tax (CGT) is charged on the donor as if the market value had actually been received.

However, in a situation where joint owners of property wish to become sole owners of part, then provided no money changes hands, a form of 'reinvestment relief' can be applied and no CGT charged.

The joint owners are treated as if each had sold their share for its market value and then the proceeds 'reinvested' in acquiring the other's half share.

If the properties are not of equal value or if one of the joint owners pays extra for a higher percentage share, CGT will be charged on the person receiving payment equivalent to the actual amount paid.

Exchange Of Interests

Alan and Brian (who are not connected persons) jointly own two rental properties, Greengables and Whitegables, respectively. Each property was originally inherited at market values of £50,000 each. They decide to exchange their joint interests such that Alan acquires the sole interest in Greengables and Brian secures exclusive title to Whitegables.

At the time of exchange Greengables has a market value of £200,000; Whitegables has a value of £250,000. No cash changes hands, but Brian has obtained the more valuable interest, and therefore greater proceeds, for the disposal of his share.

Cost for future CGT purposes = Cost of original ½ share + deemed cost of ½ share in exchange

Alan's calculation:

MV consideration	£100,000
Less cost	£(25,000)
Less 'reinvestment'	£(75,000)
Gain	NIL

Brian's calculation:

MV consideration	£125,000
Less cost	£(25,000)
Less 'reinvestment'	£(75,000)
Chargeable Gain on exchange	£25,000

Less annual exemption, if available

Cost for future CGT purposes for both properties:
    £25,000 + £25,000 = £50,000

79. Exchange Of Interests – Main Residence Problem

A form of 'reinvestment relief' is available in situations where ownership of property is swapped or is changed from joint ownership to each owning their specific part.

A significant exception to this relief is if any of the properties is, or has at any time been, a Principal Private Residence (PPR) of one of the owners or later becomes their PPR, such that a disposal within the next six years following exchange is eligible for PPR relief to any extent.

However, if all of the properties involved in the exchange become solely owned PPRs of their respective individual owners then the reinvestment relief may still apply. Married couples count as 'sole' owners in this context. The 'main residence problem' is that this 'exception to the exception' applies only if all parties' properties are their respective main PPR.

Exchange Of Interests – Main Residence Problem

Susan and Sharon jointly own two cottages, each living in one as their main PPR. They exchange interests such that Susan's house becomes the PPR of Sharon and vice versa. As no money has changed hands, the 'reinvestment relief' will apply and no capital gains tax will be charged.

However, if Susan had lived in her cottage as her main PPR but Sharon's main PPR was another property, the 'relief' would not be available.

80. 'Value Shifting'

'Value shifting' occurs when the value of a property is altered as a result of passing an interest in the property to another.

Anti-avoidance rules are in place whereby such disposals are deemed to be chargeable to capital gains tax (CGT) despite there being no consideration involved. In these situations the 'market value' rule is deemed to operate and the person transferring the value is liable to CGT based on the amount which he or she could have obtained for the transfer, if the parties had been at arm's length.

The main instances where these anti-avoidance rules operate are in the situation were the owner of a freehold property effectively changes the type of ownership by disposing of the freehold while granting a leasehold to himself or herself, thereby reducing the value of the property.

Any subsequent alteration to the lease will automatically result in a CGT charge despite no consideration having been received.

'Value Shifting'

David owns a commercial property currently valued at £200,000 with an original purchase price of £120,000. If he gifts the property to his son, with no consideration, the transaction would be treated as if he had sold at the 'market value' as the two are 'connected persons'. So he gives the freehold to his son, granting himself a lease for 99 years at a rent of £1 per year. The value of the freehold will be negligible.

He then arranges for the lease to be altered so that the rent is at the market rate resulting in the increase in value of the freehold.

The change in the terms of the lease is an example of 'value shifting' because the lease itself has become less valuable but the freehold more valuable.

At the date of alteration of the lease David will be charged to CGT on the basis that he has disposed of an asset equal to the value transferred. If the value of the £1 per year lease was £200,000 and the 'market value' lease £60,000, the value transferred would be £140,000.

The corresponding deductible cost is calculated in proportion to the value deemed to be transferred (£140,000), against the original value (£200,000).

$$\frac{£140,000}{£200,000} \times £120,000 = £84,000$$

Capital Gains calculation:

Deemed Proceeds	£140,000
Less value transferred	£(84,000)
Chargeable Gains	£ 56,000

Less annual exemption, if available.

81. 'Hold-Over' Relief

'Hold-over' relief is a way of deferring payment of capital gains tax (CGT) on certain assets, including land and buildings used in a business, until the new owner of the asset sells.

The donee, in effect, takes over the original cost of the asset and may eventually have to pay CGT on both the gain incurred from the date of gift plus the gain 'held over'.

HMRC have produced Help Sheet 295 *'Relief of gifts and similar transactions'* that details the procedure. A claim form needs to be signed and submitted. The Help Sheet can be seen at:

www.gov.uk/government/publications/relief-for-gifts-and-similar-transactions-hs295-self-assessment-helpsheet.

'Hold-Over' Relief

Judy owns a second home which shows a significant gain. She gives the cottage to her husband Jim.

This is treated as a 'no gain/no loss' disposal between them as they are married. Jim is treated as acquiring the cottage for the price that Judy paid originally (so preserving the gain in his hands), as from the date of the inter-spouse disposal.

Jim manages the property as a qualifying furnished holiday let and after a year gives the property to their adult daughter, Louise, claiming 'hold-over' relief so that Louise takes over her mother's historic base cost.

Louise subsequently occupies the property as her only or main residence such that when the property is sold full Principal Private Residence relief will be allowed.

82.   'Incorporation Relief'

Should a property letting business be run by one or more individuals who wish to transfer the property into a limited company then there will be a capital gains tax (CGT) charge on the transfer at market value.

The CGT charge can be wholly or partly postponed by use of an 'incorporation relief' ('hold-over') claim where the exchange is wholly or partly for shares in the company.

The charge is deferred until the person transferring the business disposes of the company shares. The 'held-over' gain is subsequently deducted from the cost of the shares resulting in an increased charge when the shares are eventually sold.

The business being transferred must be *as a going concern*. Should the exchange be for part shares then the CGT is partly deferred.

One of the difficulties in succeeding in a claim for 'incorporation relief' is in actually determining whether there is a qualifying business in place because the relief is not normally available on investment property businesses.

'Incorporation Relief'

The tax case of *Ramsay v HMRC* (2013) shows how difficult it is to succeed with this claim.

The taxpayer was the landlord of a large property which had been converted into ten flats, five of which were occupied by tenants.

The property was transferred to a company, in exchange for shares in that company under an 'incorporation relief' claim.

HMRC initially disallowed the claim arguing that letting is an investment activity and as such there was no 'qualifying business'.

The taxpayer appealed and the court allowed the claim, the reason being that the activities performed in the letting were over and above those which were incidental to the owning of an investment property.

Chapter 9.
Inheritance Tax Planning

83.   Inheritance Tax Charge

- Inheritance tax (IHT) is charged on the value (assets less liabilities) of a person's estate on death. The first £325,000 is exempt (the 'nil rate band') and the balance is taxed at 40% (2015/16).
- Transfers between spouses/civil partners who are resident in the UK are exempt from IHT. Therefore, if property is left to the surviving spouse/civil partner there will be no IHT due on the first death, but there may be on the second death, depending on whether the estate is in excess of £650,000 (2 x £325,000).
- If a gift of property is made to someone who is not in a marriage/civil partnership with the donor, the transfer is termed a 'potentially exempt' transfer and will only be chargeable to IHT should the donor not survive seven years. This exemption will not apply if the property gifted has conditions attached (termed a *'gift with reservation of benefit'*).
- Property placed within a 'Discretionary' ('Mainstream') trust does not normally form part of the donor's estate on death unless the settlor or their spouse/civil partner benefits from income or gains from assets held within the trust.

NOTE: From 6 April 2017 there will be an additional 'nil-rate band' available should a main residence be passed on death to a direct descendant.

The band limit will be £100,000 in 2017/18 rising to £175,000 in 2020/21. This additional 'nil-rate band' will also be available should an owner downsize or ceases to own a home on or after 8 July 2015 and assets of an equivalent value (up to the value of the additional nil-rate band) are passed on death to direct descendants.

84. Gift With Reservation Of Benefit (1)

The ideal in inheritance tax lifetime planning would be for the donor to gift the main residence out of the estate but at the same time remain living in the property. However, the 'Gift With Reservation Of Benefit' (GWRB) rules do not allow a simple transfer of a whole or even part of a property to another whilst the donor remains in residence (i.e. *reserves a benefit*). If such a transaction takes place the property is treated as remaining within the donor's estate on death.

With specific reference to land the gift would be treated as a GWRB if there is some interest, right or arrangement allowing the donor to occupy and *'enjoy the land concerned to a material degree'*.

HMRC regard a 'right' as being caught by the legislation if the right entitles or enables the donor to occupy all or part of the land otherwise than for full consideration (i.e. unless full market rent is paid by the donor occupier to the donee owner).

No GWRB applies if the freehold is gifted and then the donor either takes a lease on the property at full rent or a lease at full rent had been carved out before making the gift.

Should a sale to a 'connected person' be at a price that is less than the full market value then the balance of value will be deemed to be a 'gift'. There needs to be a sale at full market value; if not, then the 'gifted' value of the property will be included in the donor's estate on death if he or she continues to reside in the property.

Gift With Reservation Of Benefit (1)

In 2008 James sold a house then worth £100,000 to his adult son, John, for £25,000.

John did not live in the house, but James remained until he died in 2015.

The disposal is a GWRB and the value of the property gifted was 75% of the total value.

Thus, 75% of the property's value at death is treated as James' property and the value will be liable to IHT.

85.   Gift With Reservation Of Benefit (2)

The gift of undivided shares of property will not be subject to the 'Gift With Reservation Of Benefit' (GWRB) rules provided the donor and donee both occupy the property. The donor must not receive any benefit from occupation other than a negligible one, which in itself must be paid for by the donor.

It is not necessary for a proportionate sharing of the expenses of occupation but the donor must at least bear the full share of the expenses attributable to him or her.

There is no requirement for the whole of the property to be gifted. Therefore the arrangement could be as the example and be allowed.

Gift With Reservation Of Benefit (2)

James owns the whole of the house which he occupies with his (adult) daughter and son. James gifts one third of the property to each but continues to live in the property. All three contribute equally to the day-to-day expenses of the property, including the cost of a new kitchen.

If the cost of the new kitchen had been met by the children only, then there would be a GWRB at that date because the owner, James, had received a benefit *'provided by or at the expense of the donee for some reason connected with the gift'* (s104 (b) Finance Act 2004).

His daughter decides to move out of the property and at that date a GWRB will arise in respect of her share unless James pays a market rent for the continued occupancy of his daughter's one-third share.

86.   Pre-Owned Assets Tax

The 'Pre-Owned Assets Tax' (POAT) is an income tax charge levied on the 'benefit' earned on any property that has been given away (or sold for less than its full value at any time since 18 March 1986) but of which the owner still enjoys the use.

The charge also applies if the owner gives someone the funds to purchase a property, or an interest in it, or owned another property which was sold and the proceeds gifted to buy the property. The charge will not apply if there is a gap of more than seven years between the gift and the purchase of the property.

The benefit is calculated by reference to the rental value of the property, i.e. the rent that would have been payable if it had been let to the taxpayer at an annual open market rent.

There is a 'de minimis' amount of £5,000 per tax year per spouse/civil partner, but it is not possible to transfer any unused exemption from one partner to the other.

NOTE:

- Either of the Gift With Reservation of Benefit (GWRB) or the POAT rules could apply in the situation where a donor has gifted property but remains in residence paying no or minimal rent.
- If POAT applies and it is not viable to meet the ongoing income tax bill but there is less concern about the eventual IHT bill, an election can be made for the GWRB rules to apply instead of the POAT.

Pre-Owned Assets Tax

In January 2008 David gives his son, Jim, £250,000 which he spends on acquiring Greenacres. David moves into Greenacres in April 2015 and he will be subject to the POAT charge as from that date.

If the market rent of the property is £4,995 per annum and no rent is paid, there will be no POAT charge as the market rent is less than the 'de minimis' limit.

If the market rent is £10,000 per annum and David is contracted to pay a rent of £5,000, the full £10,000 will be subject to the POAT charge but with a reduction for the rent paid.

NOTE: If David had moved into a house that Jim had bought with his own money and then David gave him funds which were used for improvements, then there will be no POAT charge. The reason is that it is not David's money that has been used to acquire the property.

87. IHT Planning – Selling The Main Residence

Suggestions

- Sell the property, downsize and make a cash gift to a donee out of the proceeds. The amount of the gift needs to be sufficient to reduce the taxable estate to below the exempt amount, the remaining money being used to purchase a less costly property. The gift of cash is a deemed potentially exempt transfer (PET) for inheritance tax (IHT) charge purposes and there will be no 'Gift With Reservation Of Benefit' problems as there is no retained benefit. However, the donor does have to live for seven years for the gift to be totally IHT-free.

- Sell the property to a donee for the market price and then lease the property back, paying the full market rent to live there. The monies received could then be gifted in the form of PETs, or spent. Any capital appreciation will accrue to the recipient, the purchase money being raised via a qualifying loan. There would be practical issues such as the seller's security of tenure, stamp duty land tax payable on the sale, the market rent would be subject to income tax in the recipient's hands, and the capital gains tax Principal Private Residence relief might not be available for the recipient on the subsequent sale of the property.

88. IHT Planning – Gifting The Main Residence

Suggestions

- Gift the property and then pay full market rent to live there. The gift will be a potentially exempt transfer (PET) for inheritance tax (IHT) purposes; income tax on the rent will be paid by the donee.

- Mortgage the house, giving away the proceeds or invest the money in assets that potentially do not attract IHT, for example AIM shares. After two years, the investments should qualify for 100% relief from inheritance tax. However, mortgage interest will be charged. The funds borrowed could be gifted as a PET.

- Move to a rented property and gift the property. The gift will be a PET. If the gift is made within 18 months of the date of moving no capital gains tax will be charged if the property has been the individual's only or main residence throughout the period of ownership.

NOTE: post 6 April 2017, the suggestions given above will need to take into account the new additional 'nil-rate band' which will be available should a main residence be passed on death to a direct descendant.

The 'nil-rate band' will also be available should an owner downsize or cease to own a main residence on or after 8 July 2015 and assets of an equivalent value, up to the value of the additional nil-rate band, are passed on death to direct descendants.

89. Sales Post Death

Beneficiaries under a deceased's will are deemed to inherit the assets at market value as at the date of death. However, if a property is sold within four years of death at a lower price than the value used for the inheritance tax (IHT) calculation on the estate, that earlier IHT liability can be reduced by substituting the lower sale proceeds for the agreed value, therefore saving the estate IHT.

The relief is known as *'loss on sale of land relief'* and should more than one property be sold in the four years after death, then the sale price of all those properties is substituted for the values at death.

This relief is not available where either:

- the difference between the date of death value and the sale price is less than £1,000 or 5% of the value on death, whichever is the lower; or
- the sale is to the spouse/civil partner, children or remoter descendants, trustees or a person who had an interest in the property at any time between death and the date of sale.

Sales After Death

Molly died in September 2012 owning a property valued for IHT purposes at £400,000. The property was eventually sold to a third party for £360,000 in 2015.

The loss on the probate value is:

£400,000 – £360,000 = £(40,000).

Depending upon the value of the estate, up to £16,000 IHT can be refunded.

Calculation: £40,000 x 40% = £16,000.

90. Furnished Holiday Lets – Business Property Relief

Business Property Relief (BPR) provides full relief from inheritance tax (IHT) and is available for the transfer of certain types of business and business assets subject to a minimum ownership period. The transfer can be made during a person's lifetime or on their death. For BPR to apply the business must be carried on with the view of making a profit and be run on sound business principles.

For income tax and capital gains tax purposes the operation of a furnished holiday let (FHL) is treated as a business and, as such, it might be thought that BPR would be available for IHT. However, a recent tax case has confirmed that an FHL is not automatically treated as a business for IHT purposes and as such BPR may not be allowed (*HMRC v Pawson* (2013)).

This court decision brings matters more in line with other BPR cases and although it should not preclude all furnished holiday lets from qualifying it does confirm that in the future BPR will be more difficult to obtain; as ever each case will depend upon its own facts.

HMRC's internal guidance suggests that some claims which were allowed in the past perhaps should not have qualified and in future the level and type of services provided will be looked at more closely, rather than who has been providing the service.

91. Gifting To Charity

Relief from income tax, capital gains tax and inheritance tax is possible should a property be gifted to a charity or sold to a charity at less than the market value. The donor must gift the entire property. He or she cannot derive any benefit, neither can he or she continue to live at the property. Where property is owned jointly, relief is only available if the entire property is gifted and at least one owner must be an individual.

Income tax relief

Relief is at market value plus associated costs less any money or benefit received in return.

Capital gains tax relief

The disposal is treated as being a *'no gain, no loss'* disposal, therefore no tax is charged. If the property is sold for less than market value but for more than cost, a capital gain will arise on the difference between proceeds and cost.

Inheritance tax relief

The value of a gift to charity is deducted from the value of the estate if left in a will.

In addition, where IHT is payable on an estate, there is a 4% reduction in the rate of IHT providing that 10% of the estate has been left to charity.

Gifting To Charity

Ron is a 45% additional rate taxpayer who in July 2015 donated a property valued at £150,000 to a charity. Legal fees on transfer amounted to £1,200.

In return the charity gives him the benefit of tickets to attend their main fund-raising event valued at £300.

Income tax relief is calculated as:

£150,000 + (£1,200 – £300) = £150,900 @ 45% = £67,905.

Chapter 10.
The Use Of Trusts

92.   The Basics Of Trusts

What is a trust?

A trust is created when a person (a 'settlor') transfers assets to people whom they 'trust' ('trustees') to hold them on behalf of others ('beneficiaries').

Why use a trust?

- *Convenience* – the beneficiary may be a minor who is unable, as yet, to take responsibility for the property themselves, or the settlor may be looking for flexibility to provide for a class of beneficiaries who might not even be born at the time the trust is created (such as grandchildren).

- *Reduce taxation* – property placed within a 'Discretionary' trust does not normally form part of the settlor's estate on death (unless the trust is one where the settlor retains an interest) and as such this reduces any inheritance tax that may be due.

- *Protect the property* — this is main reason that trusts are created – in case:
    - the beneficiary turns out to be someone who cannot manage the property themselves, or
    - the property would otherwise need to be sold to pay for long-term care, or
    - to protect the property from potential bankruptcy or divorce.

Different types of trust

1. Qualifying 'Interest in Possession' (QIIP) trusts; and
2. 'Discretionary' trusts (also known as 'Relevant Property Trusts') such as:

- 'Nil rate band' trusts
- 'Charge' trusts

Under a QIIP trust, a beneficiary is entitled to the income generated by the underlying property held within the trust whereas with a 'Discretionary' trust no one person is absolutely entitled to the income; rather it is at the *discretion* of the trustees as to the distribution dependent upon the terms of the Trust Deed.

Trust planning is for the long term and can be used to secure assets, including property, which are likely to grow in value.

NOTE: Trust planning is specialist work and should only be undertaken by someone who is qualified to give such advice.

93.   'Interest In Possession' Trust

How does it work?

- The beneficiary has the right to receive an income for a defined period from the trust (usually for the remainder of the beneficiary's life) but not the right to the capital held within the trust. Thus, rented property can produce the income but the property itself remains within the trust.

- The 'interest' will cease when a beneficiary becomes *absolutely entitled* to the trust assets either on a death (for example on the death of a surviving parent or when some special condition is met (e.g. upon reaching a specified age, say, 18 years)). On being absolutely entitled the beneficiary can direct the trustees as to how to deal with the property; the beneficiary may even require the property to be transferred to him or her.

Advantages

- 'Interest in possession' trusts are a potentially useful way of providing a safe income for dependants of the settlor, whilst ensuring that the property is saved to be passed on at a later date.

- On the death of someone who has an 'interest in possession', the 'interest' comes to an end and the beneficiary becomes absolutely entitled to the trust property, but no CGT is due (but neither are any capital losses allowable).

- A chargeable gain will only arise to the trust if the cost of the property had been reduced by 'hold-over' relief on transfer into the trust, the gain being equal to the amount 'held-over'.

94. 'Nil Rate Band' Trust

How does it work?

- A 'nil rate band' (NRB) 'Discretionary' trust is created on death in a sum to include property equal in value to the inheritance tax NRB (£325,000 for 2015/16) or the settlor's unused NRB if already part-used.
- Each spouse/civil partner must own the property as 'tenants in common'.
- The surviving spouse has the legal right to occupy the property by virtue of ownership of their own half-share.
- The trustees are deemed to own a beneficial 50% share of the property which is effectively subject to a sitting tenant; the property cannot be sold because they do not entirely own it.

Advantages

- Maximum flexibility over the estate; spouse IHT exemption retained, although this point is less relevant now the unused IHT allowance of the first spouse to die is transferable to the surviving spouse.
- No problems should a beneficiary become bankrupt or die.
- If sold, capital gains tax Principal Private Residence relief is potentially available on the value of the property as a whole.
- The remaining estate assets can be left outright.
- Assets held in trust are not assessed as capital of the surviving spouse for long-term care.
- Guarantee that the trust assets pass per the donor's wishes.

NOTE: HMRC's guide to 'nil rate band' trusts can be found at: https://www.gov.uk/government/publications/nil-rate-band-discretionary-trusts/practice-guide-70-nil-rate-band-discretionary-trusts.

95. 'Charge' Trust

How does it work?

- The 'Discretionary' trust is created on the first spouse/civil partner's death by placing his or her share of the property into the trust.
- At the trustees' discretion the loan monies are given to the remaining spouse/civil partner as beneficiary. The loan is kept by the trustees as a debt of the estate until 'called in' on the death of the second spouse.
- The surviving spouse will normally have no personal liability for the charge which can be index-linked to take into account future increases in the inheritance tax (IHT) nil rate band (NRB).
- Alternatively, the charge can be expressed as a proportion of the value of the property calculated periodically thereby benefiting from any capital appreciation, or be made to track a publicly available index of property prices for comparable properties.
- On the second death the loan from the trust is repaid out of their estate. The NRB is applied to the remainder of the estate assets.

Advantages

- The property remains owned by the surviving spouse who benefits from either Principal Private Residence relief should the property be subsequently sold, or a base cost uplift if retained until death.
- On the death of the surviving spouse IHT will be payable but reduced by the charge and, if calculated correctly, to below the NRB.

96. CGT 'Hold-Over' Relief And Trusts

On the transfer of property into a trust, the original owner of the property (the 'settlor') is treated as having gifted the property to the trust at market value for capital gains tax (CGT) purposes. The 'market value' rule applies because the settlor and trust are deemed to be 'connected' when the trust comes into existence.

If the property transferred has increased in value since the date of the settlor's acquisition, then the settlor will have a chargeable gain and possibly CGT to pay. However, the settlor can claim to defer ('hold-over') the charge if the trust has been created whilst the settlor is alive (assets transferred into a trust on death do not attract CGT).

'Hold-over' relief is a way to defer the payment of CGT until the trust sells the property. The relief is not available should the settlor retain an interest in the property transferred.

CGT 'Hold-Over' Relief And Trusts

Andy creates a trust whilst he is still alive and transfers two properties into it.

The original total purchase price of the properties was £300,000; the value at the date of transfer into the trust is £500,000 – the gain of £200,000 being 'held -over'.

Four years later the trust sells the properties for £1,000,000. The trust will be liable to tax on a total gain of £700,000 – comprising the gain made whilst the properties were held within the trust and the gain 'held-over'.

97. CGT 'Hold-Over' Relief, Trusts And PPR

The beneficiary of a trust can live in a property held within a trust as their main residence and on the future disposal of the property Principal Private Residence (PPR) relief will be available.

However, if a 'hold-over' election was made on transfer into the trust PPR is denied on any subsequent sale. This is the position whether the trust sells the property or the property is transferred out of the trust and then the transferee sells.

Therefore the choice is between:

1. paying capital gains tax (CGT) at the date of transfer into the trust based on the market value and claiming PPR relief on the future sale; or
2. 'holding over' the gain on transfer into the trust, but the trust being liable to CGT on the whole gain on the final sale.

CGT 'Hold-Over' Relief, Trusts And PPR

Where a property has been subject to a 'hold-over' relief election PPR exemption is no longer available until after it has been sold to a third party.

Consider not electing for 'hold-over' relief into the trust but opting to pay CGT sooner rather than later, especially if it is thought that CGT rates are likely to rise in the future.

Chapter 11.
Miscellaneous

98.   Stamp Duty Land Tax – Multiple Dwellings Relief

Stamp duty land tax (SDLT) is potentially chargeable whenever a transaction involving land takes place, however effected, unless there is a relief or exemption. SDLT is no longer relevant for sales of land in Scotland as from 1 April 2015 – replaced by Land and Buildings Transaction Tax. In the Autumn Statement issued on 25 November 2015 the Chancellor announced an additional charge for SDLT as from 1 April 2016 on purchases of 'additional residential properties' above £40,000. Such properties will be buy to let properties and second homes. The rates will be 3% higher than the current SDLT rates.

Where chargeable, SDLT is levied such that the percentage rate used applies only to the amount that falls within each band – in a similar way as the charge to income tax. The first £125,000 is currently charged at nil rate; as from 1 April 2016 this rate will be 3% for buy to let and second homes.

Where several properties are bought at the same time, the SDLT is calculated as if one dwelling had been purchased, i.e. by reference to the total consideration.

'Multiple dwellings relief' (MDR) allows a rate to be charged at the percentage payable on the 'average value' price (referred to as the 'Average Value SDLT'(AVSDLT)) should more than one property be purchased at one time, rather than on the total consideration.

If the relief is claimed, the total SDLT is computed as follows:

1. Calculate the 'AVSDLT' i.e. total dwellings consideration/total number of dwellings.

2. Multiply the resultant figure by the total number of dwellings.

The answer is the total SDLT liability.

NOTE: the SDLT must be at least equal to 1% x total dwellings consideration.

Multiple Dwellings Relief

Ben wants to buy flats being offered at a significant discount for bulk purchase. Four flats will cost £200,000 each plus a penthouse flat at £300,000.

Without claiming MDR the SDLT charge would be calculated on the full purchase price of £1.1m as follows:

£125,000 @ 0 %

£125,000 @ 2%

£675,000 @ 5%

£175,000 @ 10%

Total charge = £53,750.

With claiming MDR:

1. Average value = £1.1m/5 = £220,000

2. AVSDLT = £125,000 @ 0%

           £95,000 @ 2%

Total SDLT = £1,900 x 5 dwellings = £9,500.

3. SDLT must at least be equal to 1% x total dwellings consideration. £1.1m @ 1% = £11,000.

Thus, the SDLT charge is £11,000, which is a saving of £42,750 (£53,750 − £11,000).

99. Stamp Duty Land Tax – Transfer Of 'Connected' Property

If property transactions are linked (which would be the situation on a sale between 'connected' persons), HMRC do not look at each transaction in isolation in order to determine the rate of stamp duty land tax (SDLT) to charge; rather the proceeds are aggregated.

Transfer Of Connected Property

John purchases a Buy To Let property for £300,000 – the SDLT will be £5,000 as follows:

> £125,000 @ 0%
>
> £125,000 @ 2%
>
> £50,000 @ 5%

If the seller arranges a deal whereby the house is sold to John for £250,000 and the garden is sold to John's wife in a separate transaction for £50,000, you might assume that the SDLT liability would amount to £2,500 on John's property (i.e. £125,000 @ 0% + £125,000 @ 2%) and the garden not be taxed as being under the £125,000 0% rate limit.

However, HMRC link the two transactions together as the two purchasers are 'connected' and SDLT of £5,000 will be payable.

100. Value Added Tax – Renovation

If a supply is not zero-rated or exempt then by default it will be a standard rate (20%) supply. The main difference between zero-rated and exempt supplies is that a business registered for VAT may reclaim/recover all input tax incurred on a zero-rated supply but no VAT can be reclaimed on exempt supplies.

The one exception to this general rule is with regard to land and property. VAT at a reduced rate of 5% applies to the following types of renovation:

- Conversions of non-residential building into a residential or charitable property.

- Projects where the works refurbish a residential or charitable building that has been empty for two or more years.

- Conversions that change the number of dwellings, e.g. the conversion of one house into flats and conversely, a block of flats back into a single dwelling.

'Residential' includes dwellings (regardless of size), and other residential buildings such as student accommodation. 'Charitable purpose' includes buildings used by charities for non-business purposes such as churches, schools, care homes and day centres.

A special VAT refund scheme allows do-it-yourself (DIY) builders and converters to also recover 5% of the VAT they incurred on construction and conversion costs. The timing of such claims is important as DIY house builders must ensure that claims are submitted within three months of completion of the project. Evidence is needed to support the claim.

Value Added Tax – Renovation

In May 2013 Andrew purchased a residential bungalow that had not been lived in for a year, intending to convert the property into a house. Planning permission was delayed and not granted until December 2014. Andrew was working on another project at the time and the building work on the bungalow did not start until June 2015. The house was finished in September 2015.

The VAT charges are as follows:

Purchase of property: No VAT charge as an exempt supply.

Renovation work: As the property had not been lived in for two years or more when the work commenced, the VAT tax charge is 5%. Building materials and certain electrical goods supplied that are incorporated into the building will attract the 5% charge. However, building materials supplied in isolation attract the standard 20% VAT rate.

Sale of property: The sale will be exempt from VAT. Should the property have originally been empty for ten years then the VAT charge could be zero-rated.

101. Value Added Tax – Developers New Build Letting

In recent years some developers have not been able to sell and have had to let out the property instead. VAT-registered developers of new build can recover all VAT charged at the standard VAT rate as the supply on sale will be a zero-rated charge.

As the VAT charge on lettings is exempt, none of the VAT paid can be reclaimed. This is because the builders are operating as investors instead of developers.

If VAT has already been reclaimed then that will need to be repaid to HMRC. However, if there is a mixture of sold and rented flats then a Partial Exemption calculation will be required. If these costs are incurred in a year in which there is no income then, under the standard VAT claim method, none will be reclaimable.

However, HMRC will apply a 'de minimis' test using a ten-year economic life in the calculation and thus permit a proportion to be reclaimed, i.e. if the properties are let for one year before being sold, one-tenth of the input VAT would be repaid.

If the 'de minimis' calculation is breached, HMRC will suggest a calculation so that some VAT can be claimed. HMRC's suggestion need not be used and if refused, no VAT can be claimed.

Value Added Tax – Developers New Build Letting

Julian constructed two properties expecting to sell at £250,000each. The input tax recoverable on the building materials was £60,000. As the properties could not sell it was decided to let instead for a period of three years expecting total rental income from both properties to be £300,000 over the period.

The 'de minimis' calculation is:

£60,000 x 30% = £18,000

HMRC suggest a calculation based on estimated sales values and estimated rents as below:

$$\frac{\text{Estimated eventual sale}}{\text{Estimated eventual sale plus estimated rents}} \times £60,000$$

$$\text{i.e. } \frac{£500,000}{£500,000 + £300,000} \times £60,000$$

This would result in £37,500 of recoverable input VAT, recoverable in the first quarter that Julian decides to let the properties.

If the property had been a corporate development the property could be transferred to that company as a zero-rated supply and as such no 'clawback' of VAT calculation would be required.

102. Bonus Tip – Retention Of Documents

By law certain documentation is required to remain in existence for specified periods of time.

For individual taxpayers, documentation needs to be retained for five years from the 31 January submission date of each year's return. This period may be extended should a Tax Return have been filed late or where HM Revenue & Customs (HMRC) has advised that it is reviewing the return.

Taxpayers are required to keep 'sufficient' records to enable completion of a Tax Return. All records and original documents should be retained as HMRC may demand to see them to verify the information declared on a Tax Return.

Lightning Source UK Ltd.
Milton Keynes UK
UKOW06f0212160216